## DATE DUE

| | | | |
|---|---|---|---|
| OCT 7 '91 | APR 1 3 '93 | | |
| OCT 15 '9? | MAY 1 2 '93 | | |
| NOV 1 8 '9? | MAY 2 0 '93 | | |
| | 6-4-93 | | |
| | SEP 0 7 '93 | | |
| FEB 1 8 '92 | SEP 2 7 '93 | | |
| MAR 1 2 '92 | APR 0 6 '94 | | |
| MAY 1 9 '92 | APR 2 0 '94 | | |
| AUG 0 8 '92 | | | |
| AUG 2 4 '92 | | | |
| NOV 1 8 '92 | | | |
| DEC 0 9 '92 | | | |
| DEC 23 '92 | | | |

GAYLORD                     PRINTED IN U.S.A.

GET A HORSE!

*also by Steven D. Price*

TEACHING RIDING AT SUMMER CAMPS
PANORAMA OF AMERICAN HORSES
TAKE ME HOME: The Development of Country-and-Western Music

BASIC

# get a horse!

## OF BACK-YARD HORSEKEEPING

by STEVEN D. PRICE

*illustrations by Reginald Pollack*

THE VIKING PRESS    NEW YORK

# PREFACE

This book evolved out of a conversation with an editor friend who had recently moved to the outer reaches of New York City's suburbs. He spoke with great enthusiasm about the rural setting, the relaxed pace, and, remembering my interest in such matters, said, "You'd be surprised at how many families keep their own horses."

I wasn't. Horseback riding is one of America's fastest-growing sports, enjoyed not only at public stables and private clubs but in back yards and neighborhood fields. Besieged by their children to get a horse, parents are discovering that maintaining one on just a few acres is both possible and practical. Barns, paddocks, and rings are cropping up in increasing numbers, and are beginning to rival swimming pools and tennis courts as home-based recreation.

Editors and writers being what they are, we started talking about books for the amateur horse-owner, for someone like my friend who doesn't know a hock from a hip but whose horse-mad teen-age daughter has started making noises about wanting an animal of her own. I remarked that books on the subject, with titles like *A Percheron on the Porch* or *An Appaloosa in Your Orchard*, tend to be more useful to the enthusiast who, having ridden for many years, now has the wherewithal to maintain a horse. These books bombard the novice reader with considerably more information than necessary, and although they have their value, what seemed more important was a book for the complete beginner. I've written this book for that audience, for families where one or more youngsters can ride but where Mom and Dad don't. More specifically, this book is aimed at the adults who will have to help care for the animal and assume ultimate responsibility for its welfare.

An experienced horseman friend made two pithy comments about approaching the subject: "Keep it basic" and "Tell 'em to get good advice." Following this counsel, I've tried to exclude material on breeds, techniques, equipment, and activities that don't concern the novice, such as braiding manes, uncommon ailments, training a horse to neck-rein, and what to wear in the hunt field. Two facets of equestrian life requiring specialized training are jumping and driving, both beyond the scope of this book. As to "advice," you will encounter throughout these pages frequent suggestions about when and where to obtain the opinion of experts—always keep in mind that "when in doubt, ask."

Here then are the bread-and-butter fundamentals:

—Initial considerations: the amount and type of land, legal restrictions, ability and enthusiasm of riders and nonriders, and cost.

—Facilities: how to construct or refurbish a barn, paddock, and ring.

—Selecting and buying a horse: what kind to get and how much to pay.

—Equipment: clothing the horse and humans, and furnishing the barn.

—Daily care: feeding and grooming.

—Stable routines: keeping things clean.

—Exercising: by riders and nonriders, and how to go about becoming one of the former.

—Kids and horses: tips for safety and enjoyment.

—Medical matters: what to do till the vet arrives.

—Communes: alternatives to keeping a horse on your own land.

—Group activities: fun and games with other riders.

What can you, a parent, expect in owning a horse? You may wake up on the morning of an important sales conference to discover that Black Beauty has broken into the feed bin. As the 8:02 chugs off, there you are giving the dumb beast a dose of mineral oil, then walking him through snow drifts to prevent a case of colic. Why undergo such aggravation? Because the pleasures outweigh the inconveniences. A horse will provide regular, healthy exercise for the family's equestrians and, perhaps more important, serve as a catalyst to draw you and your youngsters closer together. Owning a horse must be a wonderful experience, or else why would so many families do so?

Of the many people who contributed advice throughout the preparation of this book, I want especially to thank Harry Case, a mentor whose knowledge and skills as a horseman are the envy and goals of all who know him. Reginald Pollack's illustrations are more entertaining and instructive than any thousands of words could be. The Viking Corral's O.K. people, Barbara Burn and Merrill Pollack, contributed enthusiasm and expertise to the extent that, in the spirit of offering lumps of sugar to two Thoroughbreds, this book is affectionately dedicated to them.

# CONTENTS

PREFACE   vii

*one* "SHOULD WE OWN A HORSE?"   3

*two* STABLES AND STUFF   11

    The Barn   11
    The Paddock   17
    The Riding Ring   19
    Stable Equipment   22

*three* BUYING THE RIGHT HORSE   27

    Breeds and Types   27
    Finding a Horse   32
    Buying the Horse   41

*four* TACKING UP   45

    Western Tack   46

    English Tack   46

    Selection and Care of Tack   47


*five* FEED AND BEDDING   51

    Feed   51

    Bedding   55


*six* STABLE ROUTINES   57

    The First Day   57

    Handling the Horse   58

    Feeding and Watering   59

    Grooming   62

    Other Routines   65

    Stable Management   67


*seven* EXERCISING   71

    Lunging   72

    Learning to Ride   74

    Clothing   75

    Tacking Up and Down   76

    First Steps   78

    Good Horsemanship   80

*Contents*

**xii**

eight YOUR CHILD AND THE HORSE  87

    Observations  87
    Establishing "Ground Rules"  89
    Accidents  90


nine CALL ME A VET  93

    How to Keep a Horse Healthy  93
    How to Recognize Ailments  96
    Common Ailments  97
    Caring for the Sick Horse  100


ten HORSE COMMUNES: Alternatives to
Keeping a Horse on Your Own
Property  105


eleven GROUP ACTIVITIES  115

    Horse Shows  115
    Games  117
    Other Activities  119
    Using a Trailer  120


AFTERWORD  125

    Periodicals  126
    Books  127
    Organizations  128


GLOSSARY  131

Contents

GET A HORSE!

one "SHOULD

# WE OWN A HORSE?"

Not so long ago there was a girl who had just entered her teen-age years and who developed symptoms common to many youngsters of that age group. She gave up her piano lessons so that she could take two riding lessons a week after school, in addition to one on Saturday mornings. Riding boots were polished every day and rested in a place of honor in her room. Photographs of U.S. Olympic Equestrian Team members replaced those of rock stars on her bulletin board. And when she wasn't hanging around the stable, she could be found visiting a neighbor who kept a horse on his property. The diagnosis—horse-fever. The girl's parents, neither of whom had ever ridden, had remained relatively immune, involved to the extent of paying for the lessons, taxiing their daughter to and from the stable, and celebrating her birthday with a trip to a horse show. Then one day they were asked a question which changed the lives of everyone in the family—"Can we get a horse?"

That request, posed with increasing frequency around the nation, is one which any parent whose child takes riding lessons can sooner or later expect to face.

"Are you crazy?" is the typical initial reaction, followed in rapid succession by a barrage of objections: "Where would we put it?" "We couldn't possibly afford one—do you think we're millionaires?" "What if it gets sick?" "Who's going to take care of it if you get sick?" "A horse smells and his manure is even smellier—what will the neighbors say?" "What would we do with the damned thing if you get tired of riding?" These responses carry little weight with a victim of horse-fever, who has already worked out all the answers. "Lots of families in the area keep horses and those people aren't rich or live on more land than we do. I'll take care of the horse, and I'll never, ever get tired of it."

The way to break such an impasse is to examine the attitudes of your family's members and to look realistically at certain physical and financial resources. (And besides, there are alternatives by which you can still own a horse even if it's not kept on your own property.)

First of all, your family's equestrian must known how to ride well enough to do so alone, without professional supervision, as a matter of elementary safety. A back-yard facility is no place for learning-while-doing. In addition to this ability, the rider must be serious enough about owning a horse to want to ride and care for it every day. A dog can be let out of the house, a cat can create its own amusement with a ball of yarn, but a horse needs daily attention in the form of feeding, cleaning, and exercising. Few sights are sadder than a horse deprived of exercise and grooming and such negligence can make it a candidate for serious ailments. Children will profess a dedication approaching a nun's final vows about mucking out a stall or giving the horse an hour's workout every day. Despite the best of intentions, however, school functions, parties, and other attractions have a tendency to divert a child's interest once the initial excitement of owning a horse has worn off. The best judge of both your youngster's ability and sense of responsibility will be the riding instructor, along with your own personal knowledge of the child's attention span.

Equally, if not more, important is the attitude of the rest of the family, especially of you adults on whom the ultimate responsibility will rest. Nonriders must be willing to take on chores (including exercising the horse, which can be done from the ground) to the extent that the animal will belong to the whole family, not only to its riders.

Most horsemen recommend a minimum of one acre of fairly level and well-drained land for each animal. Not only is it unfair to confine so large and active a creature to a smaller patch of ground, but it also does not take much time for nibbling and pawing to turn a piece of meadow into bare soil, which one good rainfall will transform into a rice paddy. The more land, therefore, the happier the horse and the less concentrated the damage. An animal receiving several hours' worth of exercise every day can get by in a paddock of less than one acre, but certainly not less than on half an acre (approximately 20,000 square feet, or roughly within the boundaries of 200 by 100 feet). A barn will require at least another 22 by 10 feet of space (which can be a corner of the paddock); a ring for riding will use up another 100-by-70-foot area.

Although you may have enough land, you'll have to check your town's zoning laws. Most regulations prohibit livestock on plots of less than two acres. Zoning laws are changed as areas become more populated; this is not always retroactive, so the fact that someone nearby has kept a horse for several years does not necessarily mean that you can, too. The town clerk or an attorney can provide all the facts you need about minimum land as well as any additional restrictions with respect to types of buildings, sanitation facilities, and the distance required between stable or paddock and neighboring property.

Accessibility to professional care and supplies must also be taken into account. A veterinarian and feed dealer must be in the vicinity; a blacksmith and saddlery shop close by are also helpful though not indispensable (the smith, however, should be near enough to be able to come on a few days' notice). Not all vets are familiar with the kind of care a family-owned horse needs, but a stable manager or horsy neighbor should be able to recommend one who is. A feed dealer is someone else with whom you can discuss the matter of buying a horse: he can give you precise figures about the cost of equine nourishment and direct you to a bedding supplier if he can't also take care of that.

Finally comes the matter of finances. When averaged over a year or so, $75 a month is a realistic amount for a horse kept in a suburban area, with the cost dropping somewhat as one moves out into rural areas. From $20 to $45 of this figure goes to feed and bedding (the precise cost varies according to type used, locale, and season), with the balance for stable supplies and

blacksmith and veterinary bills. Initial expenses take a big bite: $250 to $750 for the horse; up to perhaps $250 for tack; and another few hundred dollars for constructing and furnishing a stable, paddock, and ring. The total may strike you as steep to the point of being prohibitive, especially with that sizable outlay at the onset. But think about the cost of a family vacation or of sending one or two children to summer camp; these are expensive, too, yet a horse is a year-round presence and delight.

*Get a Horse!*

Now for alternatives. Parents of a child still in the novice equestrian stage would be better off to consider buying a horse and boarding it at the stable where the youngster takes lessons. In that way the rider will have the opportunity and responsibility of caring for a horse while improving his skills, until he reaches the point where he can manage the animal at home without supervision. Renting a stall with feed and bedding provided is known as "rough board," and costs between $100 and $125 a month, not including blacksmith and veterinary expenses.

In the event that zoning restrictions or inadequate or unsuitable land precludes keeping a horse on your own property, look into the possibility of boarding the animal with a horse-owning neighbor who has enough space to support another animal. He might be quite pleased to have you share feed and bedding expenses (there are economies of buying in bulk); you will foot the bill if another stall must be added to his barn. If you can't find such a neighbor and if there are other parents in the neighborhood thinking about buying horses, see Chapter 10 for advice on setting up a "commune" on centrally located, suitable land.

Once you know what factors are involved, conversations with horse-owners, vets, blacksmiths, and stable managers will reveal that keeping a horse is not as impractical or impossible as you had thought. As evidence, just look around your township or village and see how many families have one. Once you've decided to buy a horse of your own and to keep it on your property, you're struck with the first question, "How to begin?" The best answer is "slowly."

As a matter of common sense, you'll have to wait until stable, paddock, and ring are built, a matter of weeks or even months. Then, too, the time of year is a factor; why buy a horse in November if weather won't permit comfortable riding or exercise until spring? Use the interim to learn as much as you can about what you're getting into. Many riding academies offer stable-management courses in the evenings, giving instructions on grooming and other basics. Make a point of watching your children ride; as you do so, you'll meet the parents of other horse-crazy youngsters as well as the stable's manager (a most helpful person to know). Stay in touch with the blacksmith and feed dealer, keeping them advised of what you're about to do. Browse around saddlery shops. Attend local rodeos and horse shows. Go with your child when he visits a horse-owner, and get to know thy neighbor.

"You" in the preceding paragraph is meant to be plural. When such excursions become family outings, everyone will become exposed to the world of horses and horsemanship, and your tribe's riders will gain confidence in showing off their skills and expertise. To make horsekeeping a family affair at this beginning stage not only sets the tone for future years, but it will also start that much earlier the wonderful experience of owning, caring for, and using a horse.

*two* STABLES

# AND STUFF

As high-pitched shouts of "We're going to get a horse!" echo through the neighborhood, your first step is to plan where and how you're going to keep the animal: to wit, building and outfitting the stable, paddock, and ring. The cost will depend on the size, type of material, and labor, although if you are a capable do-it-yourself carpenter you can reduce the total expense by eliminating the last item.

## THE BARN

Requirements for the stable/barn/shed (call it what you will) begin with location. The most practical site is in a corner of the paddock, close enough to your house for convenience, but far enough away to avoid unwanted sounds and smells. Any spot is suitable provided it has good drainage from rain or melting snow. Plan on an area of at least 20 by 12 feet.

Flooring is a barn's most important feature, for it bears the brunt of weight and mischief—horses are masters at relieving boredom by trying to excavate surfaces. Packed clay readily absorbs moisture (the way kitty litter does) and is easy on horses' legs, but constant pawing can cause you to spend too much time replacing divots. Bare dirt floors have the same disadvantage, and in any case soil isn't very absorbent.

There are some who will disagree, but concrete is a perfectly acceptable material when an adequate layer of bedding is added to absorb moisture and to cushion hooves (standing on a hard surface is as uncomfortable for horses as it is for humans). With the exception of tar, which is too slippery even with bedding, any material used as road surfacing, such as asphalt or blacktop, will do for durability and ease of cleaning, especially if there is a gradual slope of the floor toward the front of the stall for drainage.

Before the days of concrete and other synthetic stonewear, most livery stables and barns were built with wooden floorboards. Horsemen now consider that material an anachronism; wood retains moisture and is slippery footing when wet, even with bedding.

Lumber is, however, fine for walls, so long as they are solid enough to withstand the pressures of leaning and bumping and the impact of an occasional kick. Cinder blocks or bricks of several thicknesses are good alternatives. Make the roof of wood with a metal sheeting or shingle cover; if the former, a covering of tar paper will deaden the sound of rain. Aluminum siding is excellent insulation for both walls and roof (a heating system is unnecessary even in the coldest of climates).

You can avoid having to lug saddle, bridle, grain, and hay from another part of your property by allocating a portion of the barn as a tack room which also can be used for the storage of feed. Figures 1a and 1b show a plan for a simple yet comprehensive facility; Figure 2 shows its relationship to the rest of the property.

The most obvious feature of this plan is that the building is completely enclosed—highly recommended in any climate that includes snow or chilling rain (additional protection comes from having the door face to the south). Eaves extending three feet over the front and rear help keep runoff from settling around the structure's foundation.

The section for the horse is a box stall, as distinguished from a straight stall, that narrow partition prevalent at riding academies. Your horse will appreciate the additional elbow room and so will you on days when you'll have to groom him indoors. The minimum space for a full-grown horse is 10 by 10 feet; 12 by 12 feet is preferable.

The specific dimensions are aimed at safety. A minimum ceiling height of 10 feet reduces a rearing horse's chances of striking his head. So does a door set 7 feet high. Stall doors swing outward and are traditionally of the Dutch variety: the top partition can be opened for light and air while the bottom half keeps the animal inside. A window on the opposite wall is more for cross-ventilation than for observation. It can be closed by means of a wooden shutter (which also swings outward), but if you choose glass panes, make sure they are covered on the inside by heavy-gauge screening to prevent breakage and possible injury.

The tack-room area should be separated from the

*Get a Horse!*

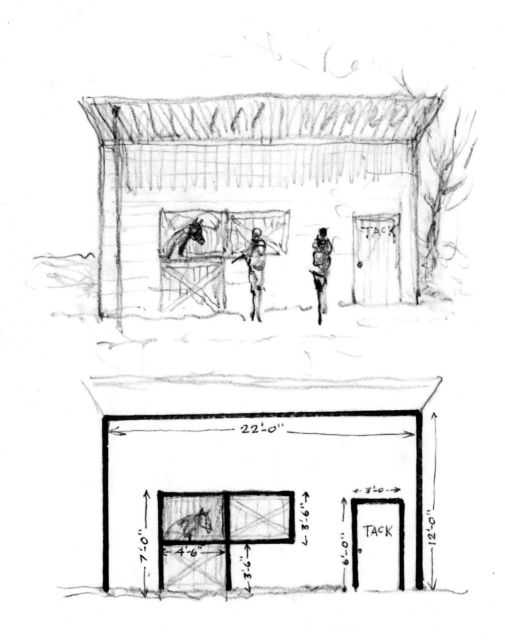

Figure 1a

14

STALL
12'-0"

TACK
10'-0"

12'-0"

5'-0

3'-6"

3'-0

12'-0

3'-0

12'-0"

10'-0

Figure 1b

15

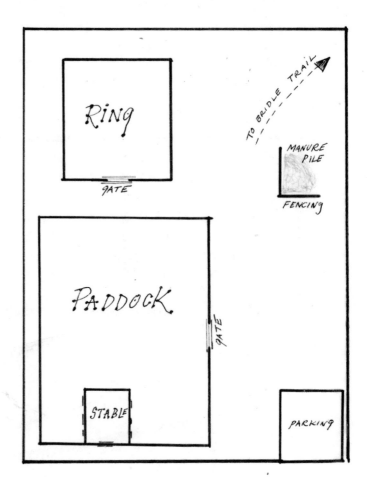

**Figure 2**

stall by a floor-to-ceiling partition as solid as the outside walls, for the aroma of hay and feed can induce a horse to try to break down the barrier. The tack room needs no windows. A cement floor will help prevent rodents from burrowing under the walls in search of food. And with regard to security of another nature, since there have been an increasing number of tack thefts recently, a padlock or combination lock will discourage thieves.

Renovating a shed or small barn bequeathed by a

former owner could prove an easier alternative to constructing another building. Consider its location, size, flooring material, and the height and width of doors in deciding whether renovation is practical. For example, an ice house of suitable dimensions to which a tack room can easily be attached may have wooden floorboards. Rip them out if they show the slightest indication of rotting (cracking, sagging, or dampness are the signs), for a horse trapped when a floorboard gives way is neither a pretty sight nor easy to rescue. If any stable requirements are absent and can't be added, it makes more sense to ignore or tear down the existing structure and start from scratch.

A manure pile figures prominently in life with a horse. Select a secluded spot within wheelbarrow distance of the barn, but not within the paddock or else the horse will become infected by parasites and bothered by flies. Keeping manure in a pit a few feet deep is tidier than just dumping the stuff. Arrange to have a landscaper, nurseryman, or farmer remove a load every several weeks, for even one horse can produce more than you could use in your garden or compost pile.

## THE PADDOCK

Be it a small paddock or larger pasture, an outside area in which the horse can stretch his legs and chomp a blade of grass or two is a necessity, and you'll find his absence a great convenience when you clean out the stall. A paddock area needs to be well-drained and free from poisonous weeds. A shade tree is always welcome, as is a running stream, so include these elements, if possible, when staking out the land.

*Get a Horse!*

There must be fencing to contain the horse and it must be able to withstand the animal's weight and curiosity. Barbed wire is the most dangerous, therefore the least desirable. Post-and-rail is attractive and also the most costly—$10 to $12 per foot. Plain wooden planks aren't strong enough alone, but the addition of electric wiring will make a more than adequate combination (Figure 3a). Sink 8-in-square-posts (8 inches in diameter if round) about 7 feet in length at least 3 feet into the ground approximately 10 feet apart around the area to be enclosed. They will support two rows of boards 8 to 10 inches wide (posts and boards having been creosoted or otherwise weatherproofed beforehand). After attaching an insulator to the top of each post, string a single strand of heavy-gauge bare wire wrapped once around each insulator to make a circuit to the power source, a transformer plugged into either a battery or the power line supplying the barn's light. Any contact with the activated wire will produce a jolt that will encourage a horse to keep its distance, yet is neither injurious nor cruel. Humans won't enjoy the shock either, so post "Beware of wire" signs and be careful. High weeds, branches, and any other object touching the wire can render the fence useless by grounding the electricity; so make a daily inspection. Unless you're familiar with such matters, have an electrician install the wiring and transformer, and give your family instructions about maintenance.

The paddock gate should be built solidly enough to confine a horse without the aid of electricity. Two types are widely used: either a swinging gate or sliding bars. To construct the latter, set the gate posts 8 feet apart, then attach two hardware brackets on each, as shown in Figure 3b. Two wooden bars 11 feet long (the excess is to prevent a horse from working them loose

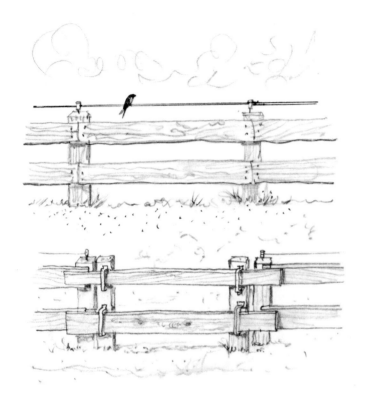

onto the ground) slide across through the brackets and can be removed to permit access. Two end posts with wooden crosspieces can serve in place of hardware (Figure 4). In either case, make sure the bars fit snugly so your horse won't be able to escape.

## THE RIDING RING

If there's no nearby riding ring which your family can use, you'll want to build one. A paddock won't do for this purpose because a horse's training continues each time it's ridden, and it needs an area that can be

*Get a Horse!*

**Figure 4**

SLIDE
THROUGH

*Get a Horse!*

associated exclusively with work. A paddock is for loafing, a ring for exercise, and the two don't mix. Neither a bridle path or a trail is an acceptable substitute for a ring, since riders will want a confined area for schooling. A workable size is 100 by 70 feet—any narrower width will make turns at the canter too tight —and the land should be flat and well drained. Board fencing without electric wiring is appropriate for the ring, as is a sliding-bar gate. Take time to remove protruding rocks and roots while you're installing the fencing.

Like Tom Sawyer sitting back to watch his cronies whitewash that fence, let me leave to you the matter of determining how much of what you'll need, then ordering supplies, pouring concrete, digging, sawing, hammering, and painting. A few words of advice, though. Avail yourself of professional guidance and services if your middle name isn't *Popular Mechanics*. Follow an expert's recommendations or hire someone to lay the barn floor and install the electric system. If you try to save pennies by buying cheaper lumber and wire or flimsier hinges and bolts you will inevitably have to spend more money on future repairs, and you run the risk of escaping horses, inconvenienced humans, and injuries to both. Painting the barn's exterior and the fencing around the paddock and ring is an attractive and useful way to reduce the ravages of weather; make sure the paint is nontoxic. In the course of construction, remove any jagged edges inside the stall and along exteriors against which a horse could rub. Finally, test the resistance of seemingly solid walls, doors, fences, and gates by heaving yourself against them. Granted, you have somewhat less power than a half-ton animal, but short of inviting the Miami Dolphins to scrimmage in the stall, throwing your weight around this way is preferable to trusting your eye and ultimately your luck.

## STABLE EQUIPMENT

On to furnishing the facility. Chores will go more easily if there is a water tap located on the tack room's outside wall and an automatic water fountain in the stall. Piping leading to the stable should be buried at least 3 feet in the ground to protect it from freezing. The fountain is about a $20 investment (plus the cost of installation) and worth every penny. It should be bolted onto a wall about 3 feet off the floor. A plunger against which the horse presses his muzzle as he drinks refills the basin, thus assuring a constant supply of fresh water. However, if you're content to fetch a pail of water, securely fasten a hook onto the wall from which a vinyl or metal bucket ($3 to $4) can be suspended at a height of 3 feet. Saddlery shops carry sturdy vinyl feed troughs for about $7, with "lips" to reduce grain spillage. Bolt one onto a corner wall for maximum support, again 3 feet off the floor. Hay can be fed from the trough, but a hay net (approximately $5) suspended from the wall at about 4 feet helps to reduce spillage. Although a horse naturally eats at ground level, dumping grain and hay on the stall's floor will expose the feed to manure residue and will allow any leftovers to become spoiled; the practice may also encourage a horse to nibble at its own bedding.

Instead of troughs and pails attached to walls, you can make two stands out of barrels or garbage cans. Fill them about three-quarters full of rocks or bricks to prevent tipping, then place a bucket in one for water

*Get a Horse!*

and a pan in the other for grain (a 6-inch-deep sink dish pan is perfect). Set them in snugly enough so that neither can be dislodged by a voracious thirst or appetite. These stands belong in the stall's corners.

Both stall and tack room need at least 150-watt lights for nighttime emergencies. A bare bulb dangling from the ceiling is an invitation to crack your head or bang a rake handle against it, so mount porcelain fixtures out of the way over each door. The power supply can come via an underground cable or a heavily insulated wire installed at least 12 feet off the ground and plugged into an outlet in the house.

The key to planning a well-organized tack room is to put everything at hand but out from under foot. Saddles tossed onto the floor will lose their shapes, so a sawhorse fitted with a broad top or a nail keg fastened to a wall can serve as a rack. Two or three coffee cans nailed to the wall are better than hooks or nails for bridle and halter storage because they help retain the shape of the leather. A 4-foot dowel or an old curtain rod between two supports would be handy as a saddle blanket or pad rack. Two metal or heavy plastic garbage cans make excellent grain containers. Their covers must fit tightly, and as additional protection against prying rodents attach a chain to one of the handles and run it across the top without slack through the cover's handle to snap it onto the can's other handle. Air circulating under bales of hay reduces chances of spontaneous combustion: place the bales on a 3-by-6-foot wooden grid made of 2-by-4s propped on 8-inch supports at each corner (Figure 5).

Tack-room tools should include a hammer, a small ax, a pair of pliers, a wire cutter, leather punch, screw driver, and assorted nails, screws, and rivets. The chore of cleaning a stall ("mucking out" in stablemen's

Figure 5

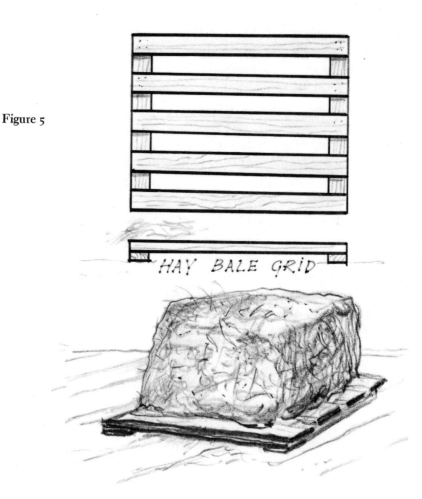

HAY BALE GRID

phraseology) requires a pitchfork, broom, rake, and a wheelbarrow with a carting surface of 4 by 3 feet. Rubber boots for family members are advisable.

While you're purchasing these implements, or perhaps appropriating some from workshop or garage, you might as well buy the assortment of brushes, sponges, and other items for grooming a horse; they will also be stored in the tack room (their use will be described in the "Daily Routine" chapter). Many saddlery shops

*Get a Horse!*

offer kits consisting of dandy brush, body brush, curry comb, mane and tail combs, sweat scraper, hoof pick, saddle soap, sponge, and rag, all for about $15.

Organize the storage space in the tack room as you would in any other workshop—you'll be busy enough without wanting to trip over a pitchfork or search for a hammer in a haystack. Tools belong on nails or brackets when not in use. Don't forget plenty of shelving space for grooming aids: an old medicine cabinet is useful for small odds and ends.

The paddock needs no more than a salt block placed near the barn and if there's no stream or pond, something to hold drinking water. The traditional fixture, a bathtub reclaimed from a house being torn down or remodeled, is large enough to save frequent refillings. Your kids might want to paint its outside with horsy scenes or psychedelic designs. And speaking of decorations, a stable's customary good-luck symbol is a horseshoe over the door, with the ends pointing up.

three **BUYING**

# THE RIGHT HORSE

## BREEDS AND TYPES

When stable, paddock, and ring are ready, the time has come to go about the business of getting a horse. Not just *a* horse, however, but *the* horse, the right one for your family's needs. Let's begin by exploring the variety of breeds and types, first eliminating those which would be unsuitable for your purposes.

Percherons, Clydesdales, Belgians, and Shires are draft horses, used for the heavy work of pulling plows and wagons. Their cumbersome size and choppy gaits make them better for hauling than riding.

Standardbreds are also used for pulling, drawing sulkies in trotting and pacing races. Since members of that breed tend to have uncomfortable gaits, Standardbreds aren't recommended as saddle horses.

Thoroughbreds are members of the breed used for

racing. Although they make outstanding hunters, jumpers, and dressage mounts, most Thoroughbreds are too "hot" and high-strung for a novice to keep and handle. Buying a Thoroughbred for a youngster would be the equivalent of putting a new driver behind the wheel of a Ferrari or an Aston-Martin.

There's still a pretty fair range from which to choose. The few words that follow about other breeds and types don't do them justice, but the books and brochures available from the breeding associations listed in the Appendix will provide detailed information.

Arabs (the breed is properly called Arabian) look fragile, on the small side with narrow bodies and slender legs, but they aren't. Arabs are sturdy and hardy, and possessed of great intelligence. Those owned by desert tribesmen come to be considered almost family members (the breed originated in Arabia and North Africa). Such affection is not misplaced, for Arabs get along well with people.

The Morgan sprang up in New England during the eighteenth century, the result of a genetic quirk. The product of two Thoroughbreds, the first sire of this breed, named Justin Morgan after its owner, was smaller and more compactly built than his parents. The versatility of Morgans has become legendary: they are smooth and sure-footed under saddle, adept at pulling a buggy or sleigh, and demonstrably eager to please. A Morgan is another strong choice for your purposes.

The Quarter Horse, usually associated with Western ranch work, is compact and rugged, made for maneuverability and quick bursts of speed (the name comes from its ability to run a quarter of a mile faster than any other breed). The Quarter Horse's tractable disposition also lends itself to a back-yard life.

American Saddle Horses, both three- and five-gaited, have been bred and schooled for the show ring, where they display elegant body carriage and high-stepping leg action. A horse so trained may be too high-strung for a novice, yet there have been several instances where Saddle Horses retired from competition have acclimated themselves to spending their twilight years in a family paddock.

Tennessee Walking Horses, which have a pleasant fast walking gait, were developed to provide a comfortable ride for Southern plantation owners when they surveyed their holdings. Walkers are calmer and more versatile than their American Saddle Horse cousins.

The Appaloosa arose in the West, where the breed's clusters of spotted hindquarter marks have long been prized by Indians. Appaloosas are sure-footed and, although associated with Western-style riding, they have proved themselves as hunters and jumpers. The Appaloosa's domesticity rivals that of the Arab.

Pintos and Palominos are really color types rather than breeds, although registries have been established for both. Also known as Paint, the Pinto has large patches or spots, while the Palomino is a golden color with white mane and tail. (Tonto's "Scout" was a Pinto; Roy Rogers's "Trigger" a Palomino). It is difficult to generalize about their size and personality because horses of any breed so marked or colored fit into these categories.

Ponies aren't young horses; they're members of any breeds or types characterized by small size, standing no taller than 14.2 hands* at full growth. Some people

* "Hand" is the unit of measurement for ponies' and horses' height, one hand being 4 inches. 14.2 (or 14 hands, 2 inches) is therefore 58 inches. Measurement is taken from the ground to the withers, the spot where the base of the neck joins the body.

dismiss ponies as being vile-tempered, ornery, and uncomfortable to ride. Not so, except for recalcitrant individuals that can pop up in any species. Consider a pony if your child is also on the diminutive side, so that rider and mount will be in proper proportion to each other. A youngster still growing, however, might discover one morning that his or her stirrups are dragging along the ground. But if that won't be for a few years, you may appreciate that a pony requires slightly less space and feed than a horse (its stall can be as little as 8 feet square). The Shetland is a popular breed, wee shaggy ponies seldom reaching above 12 hands. The Welsh Mountain Pony, with chunkier conformation, stands slightly taller. The Connemara has finer features: it resembles a tiny Thoroughbred, and grows to 14.2 hands.

It would not be anomalous for a purebred horse or pony to turn up in someone's back yard. Many have, just as some families keep purebred dogs as pets. There's the matter of finances, however: a carefully bred horse with a long pedigree can run into thousands of dollars, hardly a sum most of us can afford. Although occasionally available for less, an animal within your price range—$250 to $750—will more than likely be a crossbred or a grade.

A crossbred is the produce of two purebreds of different breeds, for example a Morgan sire and a Quarter Horse dam. The mating is sometimes planned, but more often the result comes from a nocturnal liaison between a stallion and mare occupying adjacent pastures. Breeders frequently advertise such horses as footnotes in their listings, expecting less money than for purebreds.

Just plain horses, the kind with which most riding

academies and summer-camp stables are filled, are referred to as grade. The mutts of the equine world, they come in all shapes, sizes, and colors and often display the best traits of their hybrid ancestors. As might be imagined, in a world where great store is placed in the purity of bloodlines, grades are the least expensive horses. The actual price of any horse, however, whether it is purebred, crossbred, or grade, will depend on its sex, age, training, and location.

First, there is the matter of gender. Stallions and mares of whatever lineage have a certain breeding potential, but they can also prove troublesome to control or contain when sexually aroused. It takes a strong, secure rider to keep a stallion away from a receptive mare encountered en route. Mares are easier to manage, although somewhat testy when in heat. There's also the chance that your mare may become pregnant, a circumstance with which you'll be ill equipped to deal—you'll have neither the space nor the expertise to run an amateur breeding operation. Therefore, since tractability is an important factor in your choice, a gelding (a castrated male) would be your best bet. There are many available (most colts are gelded as a matter of course) and everything else being equal, geldings are less expensive than stallions and mares.

With respect to age, any horse under five years will tend to have too much spirit or incomplete schooling to be suitable for your family's riders. Seven to seventeen years old is a good range: a horse over seventeen may be cheaper but he'll also be ready to retire before long. One over twenty is living on borrowed time and would probably be unable to carry a rider with the requisite energy (horses average from twenty to thirty years of life).

*Get a Horse!*

31

All the training a family-owned horse really needs is what Westerners call being "saddle-broke," which means willing and able to carry a rider with a minimum of fuss and frustration. Specialized schooling, such as dressage, jumping, roping, or cutting cattle, will make a horse both more lively and expensive.

Location affects the purchase price through the law of supply and demand. A horse being sold in an area where there are many others can cost a few hundred dollars less than one offered where such animals are relatively scarce. The time of year is a factor in colder climates: prices drop somewhat as winter approaches and prospective sellers attempt to save on feed bills (they raise their prices in the spring, however).

So much for abstractions. Speaking realistically, the horse you will buy depends on what's available in your locale, so here's how to go about discovering what's for sale.

FINDING A HORSE

Word of mouth is a good place to start: through a veterinarian, at the stable at which your children ride, or by telling horse-owning neighbors that you're in the market. Many family-owned horses change hands when buyer and seller meet this way. It's the most preferable method from the viewpoint of reliability, because a stable manager or a vet familiar with the animal in question will be able to point out not only its good features but also any defects or recurring ailments. Moreover, a family whose rider has outgrown a horse, is going away to school, or has other reasons to relinquish the animal is generally not looking to make a handsome profit on the sale.

Advertisements in local newspapers and "throwaways" can provide leads to available animals, dealers, and breeders, as can listings in regional and national magazines (see this book's bibliography). Saddlery shops' bulletin boards usually include "for sale" notices. Remember, though, that the majority of descriptions are euphemistic, designed to make Ol' Gluepot sound like Pegasus reincarnate. Auctions, another outlet, are better left to the professional who can size up a horse's real worth during the bidding, since few auctions permit tryouts or very close inspections. The owner of a nearby summer camp with a riding program may be delighted to lend you a horse in exchange for your footing all bills during the ten months in which you keep it. Mounted units of metropolitan police forces occasionally place retired horse up for "adoption"; New York City's will, for instance, donate horses to homes with adequate stabling facilities whenever such animals are available. Then, there's always the chance of another kind of gift horse, one which kindly Uncle Henry wants to bestow on his favorite niece and nephew. No problem if all Uncle Henry wants to do is pay for the animal, but diplomatically discourage him from showing up one morning with horse in tow, unless he's an expert on such matters or has relied on experts. If not, decline with thanks.

The importance of seeking out expert guidance in selecting a horse can't be overemphasized. There are those of us who refuse to read instructions on packages, convinced we can do everything ourselves. That's a foolish, even dangerous, attitude to have here unless you're determined to create more problems than you ever thought you, your family, and the horse could ever get into. Not just anyone who rides or has been around horses can qualify to assist you. Heed the sarcasm of "If you want expert advice, just ask someone who's

*Get a Horse!*

33

owned a horse for six months," and enlist the services of a person with a great deal more experience: your children's riding instructor, for example, or the local veterinarian, people who also would have a realistic sense of your family's requirements. When the family's needs are ignored, there can be trouble. Once, an otherwise knowledgeable fellow accompanied a family to a dealer. After looking at several candidates, he took the father aside and whispered in conspiratorial tones that one of the horses was a Thoroughbred for which the seller was asking much less than he should. "So what if it's a trifle skittish," the fellow continued, whereupon he railroaded the family into buying that particular horse. The next day as one of the children was mounting, an ice-cream truck drove by clanging its bell. The horse jumped forward, throwing the rider, and galloped off the property. Subsequent inquiry revealed that the animal had come right off a race track and had associated the bell with a starting gate's sound. The moral of the tale is that the "expert" should have known to pass up such a horse; even if it was a "bargain," it was unsuitable for a back-yard life.

Don't even dream of negotiating with a dealer or a breeder without getting expert, unbiased counsel. Horse trading is a phrase associated with getting as much money as possible, usually through the other party's ignorance and with perhaps a dollop of duplicity thrown in. Anecdotes in this regard are legion. There's the one about the dealer who fed his horses small quantities of arsenic, which gave their coats a lovely sheen and their bodies more substance. But once off the poison, the animals returned to their former cadaverous condition as the seller disappeared into the sunset. The story is, of course, extreme—and I'm not suggesting that all or even many dealers are dishonest

—merely that you're out of your league when you go it on your own.

Let's imagine a visit to a dealer who has been recommended by several of your horse-owning neighbors. You've phoned beforehand describing your requirements (including financial limits), and the dealer assures you that a selection of "guaranteed well-mannered, well-trained, and healthy" horses awaits. Your tribe arrives, expert in tow (if he isn't a vet, a doctor can always examine any possible purchase later on). As the first animal is led out, the dealer and expert plunge into the language of horse people:

"Here's a good one—a bay grade gelding, fifteen hands, just lost its cups, and safer than mother's milk. Look at those well-formed cannons."

"Yeah, but it's slightly ewe-necked and doesn't that off rear hock show a touch of bog spavin?"

"What in hell are they talking about?" you wonder, vainly trying to follow along. They're talking about color, age, conformation, and ailments.

The color of a horse's coat is a matter of personal preference, having no bearing on performance or disposition. The majority of horses are any of a number of shades of brown, ranging from chestnut (a reddish-brown) to almost black (a bay is any shade of brown with a black mane and tail). Grays and roans are colors combining white hair with other colors. Facial markings include white forehead "stars" and "blazes," the latter being white stripes extending from forehead to nostrils; "stockings" or "socks" are white markings on the lower legs. As described earlier in this chapter, Paints, Palominos, and Appaloosas have their own distinctive colors or markings. Unless your family's riders have strong feelings about this subject, bear in mind a cowboy expression that "a good horse is any color."

*Get a Horse!*

35

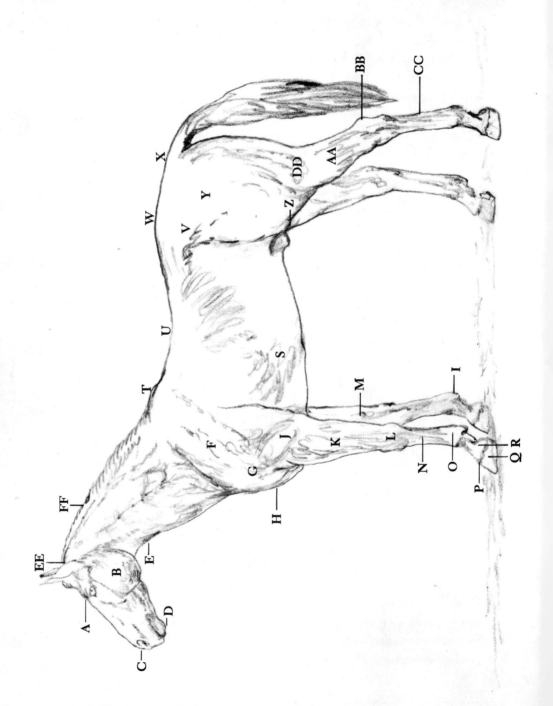

## Figure 6. Points of the Horse

A forehead
B cheekbone
C nose
D chin
E throat
F shoulder
G point of shoulder
H chest

I fetlock
J arm
K forearm
L knee
M chestnut
N cannon
O fetlock joint
P coronet

Q hoof
R pastern
S barrel
T withers
U back
V point of hip
W croup
X dock

Y hip joint
Z stifle
AA gaskin
BB hock
CC cannon
DD thigh
EE poll
FF crest

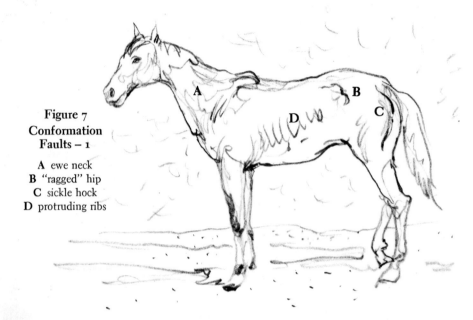

**Figure 7**
**Conformation**
**Faults – 1**

**A** ewe neck
**B** "ragged" hip
**C** sickle hock
**D** protruding ribs

Age is determined by examining the horse's teeth. To know the comings and goings of cups, grooves, striations, and entire sets of teeth is an intricate business; all you need to know at this point is that your expert is checking the horse's age when he looks into its mouth with such interest.

Conformation is the way a horse is put together, the most important criterion. A poorly constructed animal isn't physically able to perform as it should (Figures 6 and 7). Precise features vary according to breed or type, yet there are certain common elements to be found on any good horse. Here are some of the qualities for which the expert (and vet) will be looking, from stem to stern:

The head should include a broad forehead. Ears and eyes, well spaced apart, should reflect alertness and interest. Wide nostrils permit easy breathing.

The neck should be in good proportion to the rest of the body, not too long, too short, or overly arched. A ewe neck (wider at the top than at the bottom) is to be avoided, for a horse so built will carry its head in an awkward position.

The shoulder should slope at an angle of approximately 45° to the withers (see Figure 8). Since this slope determines the extent of a horse's stride, an angle of much less than 45° indicates choppy gaits, while much more means rangy, awkward movements.

Figure 8

The body should be neither overweight nor too thin —no "grass bellies" or ribs showing. A deep chest shows adequate lung cavities. Well-defined withers will keep a saddle from slipping. The back should be short (that is, the last rib should be close to where the hindquarters begin) and straight; a sway-back both looks decrepit and restricts a horse's movements under saddle. The rib area, called the "barrel," and hindquarters should show substance, with well-formed muscles throughout the latter for propulsion.

Most horsemen consider legs and feet as revealing of an animal's true value. Knock-knees, pigeon-toes, and bowlegs prevent a horse from moving well. Forelegs should hang straight down to the fetlocks for maximum support, as should the hind legs' cannon bones. Hooves must be free from ailments and solid enough to hold shoes securely (Figure 9).

One of the best indications of a good horse from a conformation standpoint is the total impression it makes. "Balanced" and "in proportion" are vague terms, but they're the way an expert would describe the sum of a horse's parts if the animal is well conformed.

The final test, assuming there's a candidate which has passed muster so far, is for manners and performance. Your expert will have taken into account how the horse has reacted to the age and conformation inspection: a mannerly horse should accept being

*Get a Horse!*

**Figure 9
Conformation
Faults – 2**

**A** protruding spine
**B** splay hock
**C** concave rib

handled with interest and without animosity, lifting its feet when asked and certainly not biting or kicking when approached. Your youngsters are the people to determine how the horse performs; they should begin by saddling and bridling him, for a horse which is head-shy or skittish for them won't be much use at home. No one else should assist them. Eliminate any animal that the kids can't manage on their own.

Does the horse stand quietly while being mounted? Will it walk, trot, and canter without much urging?

*Get a Horse!*

Are its gaits comfortable? Will the horse shy at the least provocation, particularly at moving cars and trucks? Does it have a "hard" mouth, requiring pulling and tugging to slow it down? Does it stumble or forge (striking its forelegs with its hind legs while trotting)? These are some of the questions which the trial ride is meant to answer, all boiling down to the ultimate one: do the riders like the horse?

You can be sure your children will be eager to get a horse as soon as possible. Restraining their enthusiasm may be as hard as pulling teeth, but don't capitulate if cooler heads (i.e., the expert and veterinarian) reject a prospect on which your brood has set its collective heart. It isn't the only horse in the world or even in your neighborhood, so continue to look around until you find one with which everyone involved is thoroughly satisfied.

## BUYING THE HORSE

When that animal is located, all that remains is to work out the price. Bargaining is an acceptable part of the game, both for the horse and any extras. How much more does the seller want for a saddle and bridle in good condition? Will he include transportation to your place at the time you designate? Is the down payment refundable in the event the vet doesn't give his approval of the horse's health? One of the terms of the deal certainly ought to be a trial period, a week at the bare minimum. Realizing you're a tyro at looking after a horse, any seller is within his rights to ask for an additional sum (perhaps $50 or $75) added to the purchase price since, if the horse doesn't work out, you may return it in a worse condition than you received it. It's worth the extra charge, however, to see how the horse behaves at your place. Any final transfer of title, moreover, must wait until a veterinarian of your choosing has given his approval in the event the good doctor hasn't come along with you.

For the same sound reasons that you wouldn't run your business or make any substantial purchase based on an oral contract, you'll want to have a written agreement. The wording should be much as follows:

Seller agrees to sell to Buyer the horse known as "Sultan," a bay grade gelding which he warrants (1) to be ten years old, (2) in good health and sound, and (3) to which he holds clear title. Buyer agrees to pay to Seller the total purchase price of $850 for the said animal, including the saddle and bridle taken by Buyer on this date and transportation to Buyer's house on (date), payable: a nonrefundable sum of $100 on signing this agreement; $500 ten days hence provided that (1) a licensed veterinarian of Buyer's choosing and at Buyer's sole expense certifies the said animal to be in good health and sound, and (2) Buyer finds the said animal suitable for his purposes; and $250 within thirty days from the date of this agreement. In the event either (1) the said veterinarian certifies the said animal to be unsound or in poor health or (2) Buyer finds the said animal unsuitable for his purposes, then Buyer may return the said animal and saddle and bridle in the same condition in which taken at Seller's sole expense, whereupon Buyer's liability will be limited to the $100 paid on signing this agreement, but in no event may Buyer's exercise this return privilege more than ten days hence.

(date)_____          Seller _____

                        Buyer_____

*Get a Horse!*

All this legality may sound like the Magna Carta, but remember it's for the protection of both parties (especially yours). "Warrants" is an essential word since its legal consequences hold a seller to an accurate description of the horse. Make sure that any claims or exceptions with regard to the animal's health and conditions are specified. "Certifies" is another key word, for both parties will want the vet to stand by his findings. Should the horse in question be represented as a purebred or otherwise have a pedigree in its ancestry, the contract should specify that any registration papers will be transferred at the time of final payment; such papers should also be warranted accurate. Any seller, be he a private owner, breeder, or dealer, should be willing to stand by his claims, and you're on notice of possible hanky-panky if the seller wants to conclude the deal only with a hearty handshake.

Assuming all goes smoothly, and you've made the deal, as the ink dries on the agreement and your check, something hits home—you've bought a horse.

*Get a Horse!*

*four* TACKING

# UP

It makes sense usually to wait until you've chosen your horse before getting a saddle, bridle, and other accouterments, since the proper gear depends on the animal's size and shape, as well as the rider's.

If you are lucky, the matter of tack will be taken care of when you buy the horse. That is, if both the seller and your family members ride in the same style (English or Western) and are approximately the same size, it is certainly worth the additional money to get tack in good condition to which the horse is accustomed. But if all you can obtain is a beast in its birthday suit, measure its girth (barrel circumference) and height and notice any peculiarities of conformation (e.g., narrow withers or broad back), then head for the local saddlery shop.

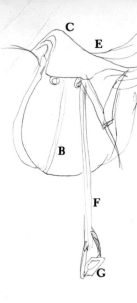

A glance around the shop or through its catalogue (such brochures are recommended bedtime reading for any horsy person) can give the less than reassuring feeling that there's no end to the number and variety of available—and necessary—items. Don't be put off by the panoply, a salesman's enthusiasm, or your family's notions of "essentials"; most equipment is either for highly specialized riding or for problem horses, neither your line of country at this point.

WESTERN TACK

Western-style horsemanship requires a stock saddle, saddle blanket, and bridle. A stock saddle is the kind with a horn in front, high cantle behind, and skirts down the sides ending in large stirrups. A Western bridle contains a curb bit, which controls speed more than direction (Western horses are trained to neck-rein, receiving signals to change direction from rein pressure on their necks). Saddle blankets are made of wool, cotton, or synthetic material and come in "pony" or "horse" sizes. As for cost, new saddles start at about $130 (including the cinch, or girth); a bridle with bit is $25 to $35, and blankets cost from $5 to $10.

ENGLISH TACK

English saddles are smaller and lighter than their Western counterparts. They come in three styles. The forward-seat saddle with higher cantle and padded knee rolls helps a rider to assume the correct jumping position. Saddle-seat riders need little more than a leather pad to show off their gaited horses' leg action.

*Get a Horse!*

The third variety is the "all-purpose" designed for general pleasure riding, including jumping (Figure 10). Fastened by either a leather or web (fibrous) girth, English saddles rest on felt or synthetic pads.

The snaffle is the most elementary bit for English riding (Figure 11). The simplest of this kind is the "broken" snaffle, two pieces of linked metal. Although there are curbs used in conjunction with snaffles (even a one-piece snaffle-curb combination called a "Pelham"), stick to a snaffle alone: a full bridle (snaffle and curb) or Pelham requires two sets of reins, and your kids will find it easier with less than a handful of leather.

A strap connected from girth to bridle is called a martingale. It restricts a horse's head elevation and offers extra control. It can always be removed if it is found to be superfluous (your expert friend can advise you about whether your horse needs one). The "standing" martingale (Figure 12) is preferable to the "running" variety, which attaches to the reins rather than the bridle, in that it's less likely to become entangled in a horse's forelegs.

Cost? Complete with fittings (girth stirrup leathers, and stirrups), English saddles begin at $125; a bridle with snaffle at $25; martingales at $7; and pad at $10.

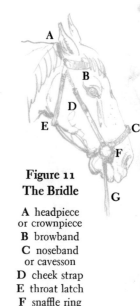

**Figure 11**
**The Bridle**

A headpiece
or crownpiece
B browband
C noseband
or cavesson
D cheek strap
E throat latch
F snaffle ring
G rein

## SELECTION AND CARE OF TACK

Whatever style of riding you prefer, the horse will require a halter. One of leather will cost about $12; nylon is equally serviceable and is a few dollars less. A blanket or sheet will be useful on cold days or in the event your horse becomes ill.

Use the data you brought along about the horse's

*Get a Horse!*

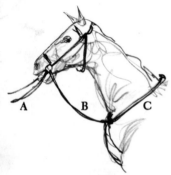

**Figure 12**

**A** reins
**B** martingale
**C** neck

size and conformation in order to select a well-fitting saddle. The animal's barrel circumference determines the size of a cinch or girth. Just as important when buying a saddle is that it should fit the riders. Choose the one most comfortable to your family's largest rider: other members will probably grow into it, and one too large for them is preferable to a saddle out of which the largest rider oozes. Stirrup irons also must fit properly: feet become stuck if they're too narrow a width. If everyone wants his own saddle you might compromise by buying separate sets of leathers and irons. The gesture will be more functional than generous, and it's a simple matter to change leathers. In that regard, a small English-style rider will appreciate an extension leather for the left (mounting and dismounting side) stirrup. Many traditionalists are coming around to accepting "offset" irons, which are built in such a way to aid keeping knees in and heels down. Small rubber pads fit into English stirrups' bottoms for greater security and support.

Many saddlery shops offer secondhand tack. As with any used item, check it for condition and hidden defects. The advantage is, of course, in saving money, and the items are already broken in. Avoid leather goods that have begun to crack. Take particular note of stirrup leathers which, if not readjusted, can fray from constant contact with a saddle's metal parts; don't pass up an otherwise good saddle for that reason—just buy another set of leathers.

False economy in purchasing tack can lead, as with everything else, to greater expense through replacement and can subject your family (which now includes the horse) to injury. Any saddlery shop should want to woo you as a steady customer and be pleased to extend a refund (or at least exchange) privilege on ill-fitting or defective merchandise. Therefore, take the purchases to the horse for a fitting by an expert as soon as possible. When in place, a bit must be wide enough so as not to pinch the horse's cheeks, but not so wide that it will rub against the corners of the mouth. It should rest comfortably in the space between the front and back teeth. The throat latch when fastened should be long enough to allow an adult's fingers to pass between it and the horse's neck. Neither the browband nor the noseband should pinch; the proper position of the latter is halfway between the cheekbones and mouth. Simply rebuckling the straps will often permit bridle adjustment, but if not, exchange the bridle for another.

The most common mark of an ill-fitting saddle is that the front arch rubs against the horse's withers. There needs to be a marked space over that portion, and the animal's backbone must not have any direct contact with the saddle. Even though your family's riders tried the saddle at the store, doublecheck it and them for size on the horse's back. Knees jutting beyond flaps or a backside extending over the cantle will mean that the saddle is too small.

New leather needs to be broken in, and almost any secondhand piece of tack can use a thorough cleaning. Knead in a generous dose of neatsfoot oil, then work up a lather of saddle soap (the saddle rack and bridle bracket come in handy during these chores). To make the leather nicely supple, work on components individually, but don't unbuckle everything at once—tack is harder to reassemble than a Jackson Pollock jigsaw puzzle. Soak the bits in clean water; they're made of rust-proof metal nowadays, but dry them with a clean cloth just to be on the safe side.

*five* FEED ANI

# BEDDING

## FEED

With his horse shot down from under him, the Pony Express rider commandeers another one grazing in a pasture. He saddles the animal with some difficulty, for its most distinguishing feature is a belly that would discourage even Weight Watchers. They gallop off, reaching their destination many miles and hours later, with neither showing any particular sign of discomfort.

A nice story but pure Hollywood. Any grass-bellied horse asked to exert itself over a considerable distance wouldn't last the route, just as an athlete fed a steady diet of mashed potatoes would hardly be a contender for an Olympic gold medal. Grass, a grazing animal's traditional forage, is fine for sustaining life and producing milk, but it lacks nutritional elements for energy and stamina. The staples of a working horse's diet should be, rather, hay and grain with occasional supplements and treats.

Hay is the dried tops of certain grasses. The grasses vary in nutritional content: clover and alfalfa are the richest in protein, too rich to be fed straight, so they are mixed with timothy or redtop (for roughage) to produce a more balanced combination.

Such talk may make sense to country folk, but what does it mean to you? Quite simply, nothing, until you've been exposed to hay's arcane mysteries, which a county agricultural agent, stable manager, or farmer will gladly explain to you. Watch how a bale broken apart falls into "flakes" of six- to eight-inch widths. Notice how much dust flies out; although a certain amount of dried soil is inescapable, too much means you'd be paying for a disproportionate amount of indigestible material. Color and texture are good indications of quality: hay should be slightly green and sweet-smelling; brown or sere means it was dried too late, permitting most of its nutritional value to escape. Hay must also be dry, for any that was baled while moisture remained can later burst into flames through spontaneous combustion or develop poisonous molds.

Hay is sold by the ton, in bales averaging 36 by 18 by 18 inches (a ton will range from thirty to forty bales). Cost will depend on location, season of year, contents, and purity. For example, the summer and fall of 1971 were bad for grass crops in the Northeast, driving the price of a ton of clover or alfalfa to almost $100, while mixed hay went for about $60. Elsewhere in the country, however, the cost was about 50 per cent less.

Feed dealers are the primary sources of hay in most suburban areas, but if there's a farmer close by, investigate the possibility of purchasing a supply from him to avoid a dealer's middleman markup. Regardless of the seller, try to buy a semi-annual supply (approximately two tons) and even pay something extra for winter storage, since prices seldom decline during winter months.

Hay is the bulk of a horse's diet, but grain provides the muscle-building portion. Like pure alfalfa or clover, straight grain is too rich; a combination of grain and hay should be fed in proportions recommended by your veterianarian. Most dealers offer oats or a mixture of oats and corn in 80-pound sacks for $80 to $95 per sack at peak prices (mixtures may also contain small quantities of bran, a natural laxative). Grain should be yellow in color, clean, shiny, sweet-smelling, and free from foreign objects.

An alternative to grain is the use of all-purpose pellets, also available from feed dealers. Pellets have been likened to vitamin-laden breakfast drinks, with, however, some of the same disadvantages. They are almost pure energy, so a straight diet of them will encourage an otherwise tractable horse to feel like challenging Man O'War. Then too, pellets are so tasty that horses wolf them down, allowing huge blocks of free time between feedings for boredom and accompanying mischief. When used in combination with hay, however, pellets can be nourishing and economical.

Saddlery-shop and feed-store brochures recommend vitamin supplements and conditioners, some of which claim to be able to turn a 998-pound weakling into a Percheron. Use them only on advice of a veterinarian, since these tonics have a tendency to make a horse too healthy; in other words, too hot to handle. Don't feel

that you'll be denying your horse anything—a menu of hay and grain will, in the vast majority of instances, provide everything a working horse needs.

"Treats" are perfectly fine, though. They include apples, carrots, salad greens, and sugar lumps, the equivalent of an ice-cream cone, bestowed when (1) you remember, and (2) you feel like being magnanimous.

*Get a Horse!*

54

## BEDDING

Even if a stall's flooring is clay or dirt, a layer of bedding makes cleaning chores easier when another substance surrounds or absorbs urine or manure. When the base is concrete or cement, bedding is essential, since hooves must rest on a softer surface. Straw, the dried stalks of grass used for hay, is a picturesque setting for a Christmas créche, but it's too costly for a year-round setting (running $40 per ton in most places). So is hay, even brown or moist hay; moreover, it's not a good idea to give a horse the opportunity to eat tainted or worthless forage. What you'll be looking for is any porous, nontoxic, cushiony substance. Many stables prefer wood shavings or sawdust. Cost depends on proximity to a paper or lumber mill, but it shouldn't be more than $150 for enough to last all year. Reprocessed sugar cane or crushed peanut shells are readily available in Southern states, while people near a large city should look into buying bags of oily sawdust used by furriers (the present price of 75¢ per 80-pound sack is a bargain for this nontoxic and absorbent material).

As with other aspects of keeping a horse, an easy and useful way to learn about feed and bedding is to pick the brains of neighborhood horsemen. The kind of camaraderie usually attributed to bowling teams and Volkswagen owners extends to horsy people, who are happy to share their experiences and expertise with novices. Don't feel shy about approaching them, tagging along while they visit feed and bedding suppliers and being introduced as a prospective customer. Your association with more experienced horse-owners doesn't have to be a one-way street, since joining to purchase feed and bedding in quantity can reduce the cost for all the buyers.

*Get a Horse!*

*six* STABLE

# ROUTINES

## THE FIRST DAY

With a coordination worthy of the Normandy invasion, you've laid in the feed, bedding, and tack before the horse's arrival. Eleventh-hour matters have been taken care of: there is a layer of bedding in the stall, and the water fountain and electric fence have been activated. A van pulls into the driveway and a few minutes later you hear the patter of hooves—your own horse's.

The first order of business is to acquaint the animal with his new home. Bear in mind that any stranger, be it a dog, cat, human, or horse, will display a certain degree of nervousness when introduced to unfamiliar surroundings. Take it slow and easy, removing anything that might prove disconcerting, such as barking dogs, sheets flapping on a clothesline, or inquisitive neighbors who have dropped by for the "debut." The newcomer may be hungry or thirsty: show him the water fountain or the filled bucket and feed bin and hayrack. Don't be surprised, however, if the horse shows little inclination to eat, since apprehensiveness can reduce his appetite. Then permit the animal to explore his domain. At some point he'll brush against the electric fence, recoiling more out of surprise than pain and quickly learning to respect the enclosure.

In spite of cries of dismay from your family's riders, wait until the horse seems thoroughly relaxed in his new quarters before letting him be ridden. There's no reason, however, not to make a restrained fuss, petting and reassuring him (and as long as we're all becoming so chummy, why don't we refer to your horse by a name—how about "Sultan," as we called him in that sales agreement?). These first few hours are also a good time for your first ground-school lesson in horsemanship.

## HANDLING THE HORSE

Horses are always led, saddled and unsaddled, and mounted and dismounted from their left side. It's a matter of tradition dating back to the days when men wore swords on their left hips (in that world of dextrous, adroit righties); knights and cavaliers found mounting and dismounting from the left easier than becoming entangled in a scabbard. Horsemen call the left the "near" side and the right the "off" side, and perpetuate the tradition by saying: "The left side is the right side, the right is the wrong side."

It is easier to catch and control a horse that is wearing a halter, and it's no inconvenience for Sultan to wear one when he's not in a bridle. The apparatus is simplicity itself: the animal's muzzle goes through the "circle," then the remaining strap snaps or buckles over the head. A lead line, which need be nothing more than a 4-foot piece of stout rope with a swivel snap securely tied to an end, snaps onto the halter ring under the chin. Everyone should take a turn leading Sultan around the paddock: stand on his left side next to his head, your right hand holding the rope about one foot from the halter while your left holds the rest of the rope to prevent it from trailing on the ground (wrapping it around your hand could cause you to be dragged if Sultan shies). Walk straight ahead, gently tugging in the event Sultan is reluctant to follow (the same technique applies to leading a horse wearing a bridle; reins pulled forward over the head become the lead line). Never turn to face a horse and pull, for he'll only dig in his heels. And speaking of heels, be careful that you don't get stepped on. This caution may sound silly, yet novices who are concentrating on leading a horse sometimes forget about that possibility. Walk far enough away from Sultan; if he comes too close to your feet, extend your right hand and push his head away by means of the rope.

## FEEDING AND WATERING

Responsibility for caring for Sultan begins this first day. It is most important to maintain a schedule of who does what when. In a family of four, one of the children can take the morning tour of duty; Mom the noon feeding; whoever will ride that afternoon handles the chores connected with exercise; and Dad is on duty during the evening (an adult should always be responsible for making sure that doors and gates are locked at night). Stick as closely as possible to whatever schedule you devise so that routines become habit-forming. Trading off assignments becomes inevitable because of illness and unavoidable absences, so everyone in the family should be familiar with all the chores. It's up to everyone, too, to keep an eye out for dwindling supplies. Never put off reordering feed until you're down to the last bale of hay or a half sack of grain; although you can probably borrow a ration of oats from a neighboring horse-owner in an emergency, doing it too often will be considered a nuisance.

Horses are highly conditionable creatures of habit, a fact you'll discover during Sultan's first few days with you. If he doesn't respond to your call to breakfast, rather than chase him around the paddock like a madman, just stand near the stall door and whistle or bang against a pail. Curiosity compounded by hunger will overcome Sultan and he'll walk up within halter-grabbing distance. Lead him into the stall, closing the bottom half of the door once he's inside, and give him his feed. After the procedure is repeated several times, you will find him waiting impatiently every morning. Encourage Sultan to come when called, rewarding his obedience with a lump of sugar, piece of carrot, or a friendly pat on the neck.

The closest we can come to duplicating natural equine grazing patterns is to feed horses several times a day. Three feedings are sufficient: morning, noon, and night. If, for example, your veterinarian recommends eight quarts of grain per day, divide it into thirds, or perhaps three-, two-, and three-quart portions. The proper amount, as the vet will explain, depends on

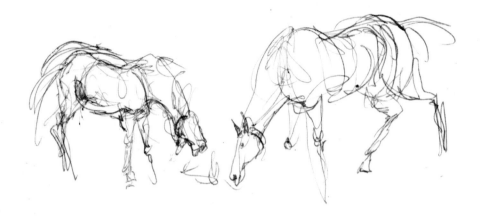

such factors as the horse's size and condition, amount of exercise, and the kind of grain or pellets. A change of diet (e.g., from grain to pellets) should be made gradually, even if you must buy a small quantity of the former—the expression "strong as a horse" does not apply to its stomach, a mechanism particularly sensitive to departures from accustomed nourishment. A treat of an apple or carrots can be added to the evening feeding of grain and hay. This chore is also the time to double-check gates and door latches and feed-bin covers. Take nothing for granted, for otherwise the tack room or a neighbor's lawn will be certain to play host to a nocturnal invader.

A horse that has no access to fresh water via an automatic fountain or running stream should begin meals with a drink. (The stomach retains solid food in such a way that a drink after grain or hay will cause bloating, which too often leads to colic.) While Sultan is drinking as many bucketsful as he wants, pour out the ap-

*Get a Horse!*

propriate quantity of grain or pellets. Carry the feed to the stall in a clean coffee can or pail; there's no need to risk spilling a heavy sack of grain en route. Sultan may tend to wolf down his grain, so it may be a good idea to give him hay first. However you arrange the courses, examine the flakes of hay for mold and other foreign objects, shaking the hay to eliminate dust.

Weather permitting, turn Sultan out into the paddock after he has eaten so you can muck out the stall. Scoop up manure with the pitchfork, leaving as much bedding material as possible. Break up and respread urine-soaked lumps of bedding so it can dry out. Transport waste material to the manure pile in the wheelbarrow, stopping off in the paddock to pick up any manure found there.

## GROOMING

Sultan will become more placid after breakfast, a good time for a light grooming. Prevent him from straying about by tying his lead rope to a hook mounted on an outside wall, then position yourself so that he is between you and the wall. Cross-tying will restrain him even more; one rope is fastened to the wall and another to a post securely sunk into the ground ten feet away.

Start by cleaning the hooves (Figure 13). Getting Sultan to lift his legs isn't too difficult it you go about it as follows: start with the near foreleg (that's the left front). Standing close to the leg and facing toward the rear, run your left hand down the leg. When you reach the fetlock, lean against Sultan to force him to shift his weight, simultaneously lifting the leg—without twisting—to get at the hoof's underside. Hold the leg

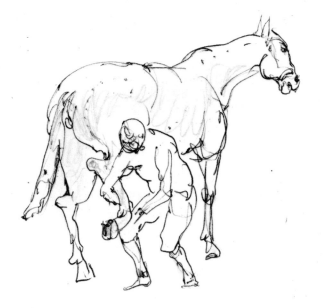

Figure 13

just below the fetlock in the palm of your hand and use the hoof-pick in your right hand. Work from the back of the hoof toward the front to scrape away packed mud and manure and any small stones. Be careful not to injure the soft midsection, called the frog. You can free your left hand by resting the leg between your knees—Sultan may fidget but he isn't balanced enough to object any more strenuously. As you clean all four hooves, check for cuts or any swelling or infection of the frog. Notice, too, whether any shoes are loose or worn; either condition will require the blacksmith's immediate attention.

Like the nightly hundred strokes a woman gives her own mane, grooming a horse has its cosmetic value, although more important is the skin stimulation which reduces dermatological problems. Morning rubdowns

*Get a Horse!*

can be brief but earnest brushings with the currycomb and dandy brush to remove the night's accumulation of dirt. Brushing in the direction in which the hair grows, work from head to tail. This feeding-mucking-grooming process shouldn't take more than twenty minutes, perhaps slightly longer until you get the hang of it.

Sultan should also be cleaned both before and after being ridden. A pre-ride once-over-lightly is necessary to remove dirt and to smooth the hairs under the saddle to reduce the likelihood of saddle sores. A quick hoof inspection will reveal any small rocks lodged there which could produce lameness. After exercise is the time for a thorough grooming. Another hoof cleaning, and it's back to the currycomb and dandy brush: begin on the face, then do the neck, forelegs, body, hindquarters, and hind legs, in that order. A circular motion of the currycomb loosens dirt, mud, and loose hair, while short strokes of the brush (ending in an upturn) remove the filth. Brush vigorously everywhere except over the sensitive parts of the face, ears, and inside legs, and don't forget such out-of-the-way places as fetlocks, chest, and under the tail. The body brush's bristles are softer than those of the dandy brush, and will give Sultan a nice sheen for a finishing touch. Clean the brushes and comb as you go along by scraping them together and knocking out the dirt and accumulated hairs.

Caring for the mane and tail is the next step. Although using a brush on these hairs may seem reasonable, it tends to break them and yank them out, so use combs instead. You won't need to worry about Sultan's mane if it has been "roached," or clipped short into a "crewcut." The decision to roach a mane is primarily an aesthetic one, although it is easier to care

for than a full mane. (One good practical reason for leaving a mane full-grown is that even the most experienced horseman has been happy to be able to grab a handful of hair when off balance.) Rather than comb in long, sweeping motions, separate the strands and do a few inches at a time to remove kinks, knots, and burrs. Use your fingers for stubborn objects, never scissors. Sultan won't object to pulling and tugging, since there are no nerve endings at the mane and tail roots.

Finished. Stand back to admire your efforts, then let Sultan loose in his paddock and watch that equine ingrate make a beeline for the nearest mud puddle or patch of bare soil to roll over in.

## OTHER ROUTINES

Once-a-week chores include changing the bedding and washing the stall floor (sweep out excess water before replacing the bedding), and cleaning and polishing all tack (more frequently if they become encrusted with dirt). Set a time for this heavy work so that everyone can pitch in.

Weather will affect a horse's grooming requirements. Humans bathe or shower in the summer for cleanliness and relief, so why not Sultan? Add a little of the shampoo your family uses to a bucket of warm water, then swab the horse with a large sponge (also the method of removing grass and manure stains any time of year). Keep soap out of his eyes, and change to clean water once you've gone over soiled areas. Remove excess water with a sweat scraper and a wrung-out sponge; follow this by walking the horse around the paddock until he is thoroughly dry, to keep him from rolling on the ground or standing in a draft while he is still damp. Summer heat will also cause a delay in some of the chores: watering or feeding a horse which is hot after exercise is *verboten*. While being ridden or just roaming the paddock, Sultan will appreciate generous applications of insect repellent. Access to a salt block in either the stall or paddock is beneficial any time of year, but particularly during summer days when sweating causes a loss of salt.

Winter's colder days call for periodic checks to see whether water in buckets or in the fountain and pipes has frozen; you may have to fetch a pail of tepid water if it has. Most horses grow heavy coats of hair as this season approaches. The coats retain sweat during and after heavy exercise, a situation that can lead to colds. Clipping, a way to guard against it, should be done only on advice of your vet. If he recommends it, have someone familiar with the procedure do the clipping: novices tend to injure the skin or cut uneven swathes through the shag. A clipped or thin-skinned horse should wear a blanket (sometimes called a rug) in an unheated stable; blanketing retards the growth of the thick hairs. Measure Sultan's length from the point of shoulder to tail and his girth to help the saddlery-shop clerk determine the correct blanket size.

Rainy days any time of year will force you to alter schedules. Manure should be removed several times a day whenever a horse spends more time indoors, and riding or lunging after a downpour calls for extra effort in cleaning a bespattered animal, a chore made easier by waiting until the mud has dried.

## STABLE MANAGEMENT

All these chores will be less formidable if you learn the fundamentals of stable management before you acquire your horse. In the event the local riding academy doesn't offer a course, just hang around there or with a horsy friend or neighbor. Ask questions, and don't be shy about trying your hand with a dandy brush, hoof-pick, or manure rake. The horse-owner will be pleased by the help and you'll develop the necessary skills. Consult a chart posted in your tack room until routines become second nature so you won't forget anything: that list might include, for example, all the steps in grooming Sultan. Once again, seek expert advice. Let the vet, blacksmith, feed dealer, and others familiar with horses know what you're doing, and heed their suggestions. Saddlery shops are another source of guidance; if you view with a slightly jaundiced eye any persistence in urging you to buy something, remember that they know they'll lose your patronage by selling you unnecessary items.

The following five "commandments" are universally accepted for efficiency and safety:

—Keep tools and other implements within handy distance during chores. It's both boring and a waste

*Get a Horse!*

67

of time to have to go back for a forgotten comb or sponge. Replace all items as soon as you're finished so they'll be there the next time you need them.

—Always let Sultan know when you're approaching him, coming from the front whenever possible and speaking in calm tones. Don't take it for granted that he sees you—horses can doze on their feet. Wait until he acknowledges your presence by a whinny or an ear or eye movement before you handle him.

—To pass close behind a horse, especially during hot, fly-ridden weather, is to chance a kick. Ears flattened back or a cocked hind leg are warning signs of trouble afoot. The extra steps to walk around Sultan's head or a few yards behind can prevent a careless injury.

—Never, ever, tie Sultan by the reins, no matter what the Lone Ranger might do. They're not strong enough to restrain his full weight; then, too, a strong wrench on the bit can damage a horse's mouth. Use a halter or make one using a rope: tie one end around the horse's neck (knotted so it won't choke him) and slip a loop over his muzzle.

—Smoking around a stable area is a cardinal sin. Hay and bedding are highly combustible, and horses react violently to flame and smoke. Keep a Fire extinguisher in good condition handy.

The first week of riding and caring for Sultan is the period in which to determine whether he is worth keeping. If you arrive home from work to find Junior with his arm in a cast, Sis in tears, and the horse in the flower bed, the omens are not good. Be hard-nosed about the decision; it's no reflection on anyone if a horse thought to be suitable turns out to be too difficult for novices to manage. In that case, exercise the return or exchange privilege, or plan to sell Sultan—

just find a more appropriate horse without becoming soured on the idea of owning one. Chances are good, however, that through the combined efforts of your family and friends, Sultan (or Buttermilk or Whatever-the-Name) will provide many years of fun and happiness, beginning on the day he arrives.

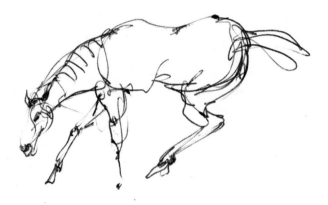

seven

# EXERCISING

The time spent exercising Sultan will be the high point of the day, the chance for riders to work out in the ring or disappear down a nearby trail, the *raison d'être* of owning a saddle horse. Because exercise is so enjoyable a "chore," there should be no problem in locating others to substitute in the event your youngsters are ill or otherwise unable to ride. Their friends and neighbors will probably clamor for the privilege, which should be granted only to those who ride well enough and have obtained their parents' consent.* Be sure to determine from your insurance broker, in any

---

* Capable and responsible "backup" riders are people whose services you'll want to enlist to look after Sultan when your family is off on vacation. Working out a reciprocal arrangement with another horsy family is another common "horse-sitting" technique.

case, whether your policy covers injuries to strangers. Should no one else be available, however, the responsibility of exercising the horse rests with you, as parents.

## LUNGING

Don't panic—there is a method for Sultan to receive his daily constitutional without your having to leave the ground. It's called lunging (pronounced with a soft "g"), a procedure in which the horse, controlled by a long rope attached to his halter, moves in a circle around you. Some training will be required, certainly for you, so start this schooling soon after Sultan arrives. Equipment consists of a 25-foot length of stout rope with a snap fastened to one end and a 5-foot whip with a long lash (a springy branch or old fishing rod with a piece of packing twine tied to the tip will do equally well).

With someone else to assist you, lead Sultan to the ring and snap the lunge rope to the halter under his chin. As your assistant holds the horse near the rail, walk to the center until about 20 feet of rope separate you and Sultan. Standing beside the horse on the rail side, your helper leads him around at a rapid walk while you hold the rope to the horse. Hold the rope in your hand closer to his head (the left if Sultan is moving counterclockwise), but don't wrap it around your hand or you may be dragged if the horse shies or bolts. The whip belongs in your other hand, pointed several feet behind Sultan with the tip a few feet off the ground (Figure 14). After three or four revolutions, ask the helper to release Sultan's head.

Perhaps Sultan has realized that he's supposed to

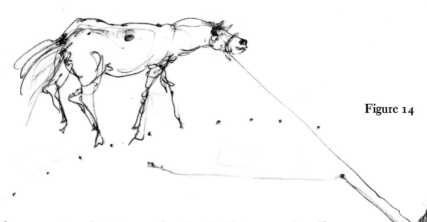

Figure 14

keep moving, but it may be that he'll turn and walk toward you. Make him keep his distance by pointing the whip at his chest and urge him ahead by gently flicking the lash at his hind legs (a maneuver combining elements of saber-wielding and fly-casting). Remember that the whip is never used as punishment but only as a signaling and guidance device. If used properly, the whip should not frighten the horse, and this goes for riding crop and spurs as well. If Sultan still insists on walking up to you, ask your assistant to lead him back and start him off again (too much pressure on the rope can encourage a horse to move in; a light contact is all that is required). Under no circumstances should Sultan stop on his own: flick the whip under his nose to make him halt, then walk up to him without reeling him in. Once Sultan is going well at the walk, stop him and reverse direction, switching rope and whip hands. The signal to trot is a clucking sound while you flick the lash against his hind legs. If the horse bolts or otherwise goes out of control, wait until he slows down to an easy trot (drop the rope if you're about to be dragged), then begin again.

Several short sessions should accustom Sultan and you to lunging. When there's no one available to ride,

*Get a Horse!*

73

lunging for thirty to forty-five minutes will give the horse sufficient daily exercise. Vary between walking and trotting in both directions (cantering will be too difficult to control). Always keep Sultan going at a brisk pace, not merely ambling—remember, this is exercise.

## LEARNING TO RIDE

After you've been around Sultan for several weeks, gradually losing any reticence about horses, don't be too surprised if you catch yourself wondering whether you, too, could ride. The answer is a resounding yes—there's no age limit for beginners. Try it!*

Many books contain detailed information about do-it-yourself horsemanship. The instruction may be clearly and accurately written, but there are three reasons why taking lessons is a better idea. You'll learn more, and therefore be able to do more. An analogy to skiing may be apt: a lifetime of snowplowing down novice slopes is possible but rather boring. Next, teaching yourself will inevitably lead to bad habits on the part of both you and the horse, which in turn will spoil Sultan's schooling. Your kids should be encouraging you to take lessons for this reason alone. Finally, as in any sport involving an element of risk, qualified instruction reduces the chance of injury. Look into evening or weekend classes at the local riding academy (adult-education programs in many schools offer riding) or else your family's riders can teach you.

On the assumption that you won't be teaching your-

* The only horsefly in the ointment may be your size. A person weighing more than 200 pounds or standing over six feet will find riding a pony or small-boned horse as uncomfortable as the animal will feel being ridden. Check with a vet or stable manager if there's any question about whether Sultan can carry you.

self, this chapter won't be a how-to manual in the sense of "put your left leg in the left stirrup" since such guidance will fall within your instructor's bailiwick. Let's confine ourselves, rather, to certain abstractions, rules, and safety tips applicable to all styles of riding.

Your first lesson can be simply watching Sultan move freely around the paddock. Notice that he's a "rear-engine" vehicle, receiving his power from his hind quarters, which "push" the rest of his body ahead. Head and neck act as balancing devices, extended in relation to his speed. Then watch one of your family in the saddle. A rider's role is to interfere as little as possible with these natural movements, at the same time transmitting signals to request and control gaits, direction, and speed. You'll be pleased to discover that brute strength has nothing to do with riding; how else could small children manage animals outweighing them up to twenty times? The secret is balance, used both to stay in the saddle and to control the horse through leverage and coordination.

## CLOTHING

A word or two about clothing. Boots and breeches or jodhpurs if you ride English-style, or high-heeled boots if Western, are proper and useful, yet expensive, investments. Start off by wearing tight-fitting pants to avoid chafing (blue jeans are fine) and any kind of boots or laced shoes so long as they have heels. Heels prevent feet from slipping through stirrups, so sneakers won't do, and loafers or moccasins don't provide enough support. Your family's riders should have protective caps of the fox-hunting variety, and if one of theirs fits you, wear it.

*Get a Horse!*

## TACKING UP AND DOWN

Suitably attired, head for the barn and your first instruction session. Novices find tacking (saddling and bridling) an intricate procedure, so watch closely as it is done preparatory to your ride. The following guide will be helpful to have handy until you've memorized and practiced the steps:

Leave the saddle, with pad or blanket, on a gatepost, stall door, or the ground (if the last, standing on its end, cantle, or back end, up) until it's needed. Hold the reins in your right hand and the bridle by its crownpiece in your left. Slip the reins over Sultan's head. Still holding the bridle, unbuckle and slip off the halter—the reins around the neck can offer sufficient restraint in case the horse decides to wander away. Transfer the crownpiece to your right hand and draw Sultan's head down to your level with your right arm behind his ears (press your left hand against his muzzle for added emphasis if necessary). Squeeze the back of the jaw where the lips begin with your left hand to force Sultan's mouth open—there's no danger of being bitten since horses have no teeth in that spot. Insert the bit the moment he opens his mouth to protest this labial indignity, then quickly maneuver the crownpiece over his ears (Figure 15). Pull strands of forelock hair through the browband. Buckle the throatlatch, allowing enough room to pass your flattened hand between that strap and Sultan's neck.

Slip the reins forward over Sultan's head so you can lead him as you fetch the saddle, or else buckle the halter loosely around his neck to moor him to the hitching hook. If you're using a Western saddle, fold the blanket in half and place it on Sultan's back just behind the withers, fold side toward the horse's head.

Figure 15

Make sure it's smooth, for wrinkles can cause saddle sores. Grasp the saddle horn in your left hand and cantle in your right. Place (not plop) it onto the blanket, trying not to tangle girth and stirrups underneath. Reach under the belly for the girth and run the cinch strap through its ring, then back through the cinch ring, making sure that the girth isn't twisted. The cinch knot is a kind of cloverleaf: across to the left, under and across the ring to the right, then under the ring and through the loop formed by the cinch strap. The knot must be securely tied.

An English saddle is easier to lift and fasten. The pad goes on first, fitting as a blanket does smoothly across the back. Place the saddle over it in the same manner as a Western saddle. Reach under for the girth, see that it's not twisted, then buckle it to two of the billet straps under the flap (most saddles have three billets: use the outside ones, leaving the middle as a spare). There is a tendency among novices to

*Get a Horse!*

77

fasten a girth too loosely: the correct tension is achieved when your flattened hand can barely pass under it. Many horses puff out their bellies while being saddled, a trick they learn in order to reduce the tension. If you suspect this is one of Sultan's little jokes, either wait for an exhalation or poke him in the ribs, then quickly tighten the girth.

A standing martingale goes on as follows: unbuckle the bridle's noseband; insert the martingale's smaller loop so it is positioned behind the jaw; then rebuckle the noseband. The beltlike hoop buckles around the horse's neck, and the martingale's larger loop passes between the forelegs onto the girth (placed there, of course, before the girth is fastened).

Removing saddle and bridle is pretty much the reverse of the above. Flapping stirrups are a nuisance and a danger; before unsaddling, run English stirrup irons up the back strap of the leathers, then tuck the leathers through. Unknot or unbuckle the girth (slipping the martingale loop off the girth; there's no need to detatch it from the bridle), and remove the saddle and pad or blanket. As for the bridle, unbuckle the throatlatch, then pull the martingale neckstrap and crownpiece over Sultan's head with one hand—the horse will be more than pleased to cooperate by spitting out the bit. Reins are removed last; they should remain over the neck until the halter is refitted.


FIRST STEPS

Up at the ring, if Sultan is feeling frisky, your instructor should ride for a few minutes to get the bucks out. When you're ready to mount, have the instructor grasp the right stirrup to brace the saddle and hold the bridle to prevent the horse from moving. Up you go. Now the stirrup leathers are adjusted. Your feet must be able to slip easily into them, so buy a set of your own if you don't fit the ones for your child. Your instructor will show you how to hold the reins and the fundamentals of body and leg position.

As you're being led around at a walk by means of a lead rope, try to become accustomed to your altitude and to Sultan's motion. This initial lesson should concentrate on learning form and basic control, which involves starting, stopping, and changing direction. Twenty or thirty minutes may be all your concentration and muscles can take—don't force yourself to ride beyond your limit. Now you've earned a muscle-relaxing hot bath and a cold drink.

During the next few sessions, focus on developing form and building confidence. You will soon be able to start, stop, and change directions at the walk without a lead rope. You'll find that squeezing your lower legs against the girth will urge Sultan forward; horsemen call it "engaging the hindquarters."

Nothing is more discouraging at this stage than to hear constant reminders to "keep your heels down!" "knees in!" and "stop leaning on the reins!" No one expects you to acquire all the elements of form at one sitting, so just relax and—oh yes, keep your heels down, knees in, and reins in gentle contact with Sultan's mouth.

The trot is the next gait to master. Western-style, it's a transition between the walk and lope, to which riders sit by absorbing the impact in the lower backs and legs. The more relaxed you are the easier it will be. Trotting in the English fashion involves posting, which is raising and lowering your body at each step in a kind of controlled bounce. Since posting is a matter of rhythm, try humming a tune to help you find the pattern—"Hail, Hail, the Gang's All Here" works well.

The canter, called the lope by Westerners, is a three-beat gait to which you'll sit no matter which style you ride. A horse cantering in the ring must be on the correct lead, a term which describes the order in which his feet strike the ground. Watch Sultan as your instructor canters him and notice that when he's going counterclockwise, his left foreleg strikes the ground last. This order permits a horse to support himself on his inside leg. A combination of rein and leg pressure indicates the correct lead, and once the horse has broken into that gait, the rider then keeps his arms and wrists flexible for a steady contact with the bobbing head movement. Like posting, sitting to a canter requires getting into the rhythm, and like sitting to a trot, it's easier if you relax and keep your lower back flexible.

## GOOD HORSEMANSHIP

A feeling of pride is quite justified on that day when your instructor pronounces you a rider. The time needed to develop the skills depends on your aptitude and the numbers of hours spent in the saddle—as in any sport, it's a matter of practice and perseverance. But don't think that once you've learned form and control you'll ride perfectly every time out: part of each ride involves loosening up and regaining balance and coordination, especially after a layoff of a week or so.

The balance of this chapter, a mixed bag of aphorisms, explanations, and safety tips, may help you to become a confident and knowledgeable rider a little more rapidly.

Someone has an "independent seat" when he can stay in the saddle without needing to rely on the reins for support. Avoid the tendency, for example, to pull on Sultan's mouth to lift yourself while learning to post. A secure, "independent" seat comes from balance and contact with the saddle, not from squeezing or wrapping your legs around the animal's belly. Severe rein pressure, moreover, both confuses a horse and restrains him from moving forward.

"The rider's hands belong to the horse" is a maxim easier to fulfill after you've developed an "independent seat." By that is meant the sensitivity needed to maintain a steady, constant contact with the horse's mouth without restraining his forward movement. Except to slow the horse down, your hands should flow with the animal's head motion; the motion is analogous to the give-and-take technique used to reel in a fish. Work toward the highest accolade a rider can receive: "generous" hands.

Yelling, cursing, or otherwise betraying fear or nervousness are invitations to trouble. Horses are quick to pick up human emotions and they act accordingly. Stay calm when you're in the saddle (or any other time around animals). Anger, too, is dangerous and cruel. A horse is a sensitive, living creature—never make him the object of your frustration when something goes wrong, as you might a tennis racket or golf club.

But never let a horse gain the upper hand. You're the one to determine where and at what speed you're both going. Don't capitulate if Sultan decides to cut across the ring, stop and graze, or head for the barn sooner than you wish. Move him ahead by engaging his hindquarters and point him in the desired direction by a combination of rein and leg pressure. You can resort to using a crop for emphasis if you fail to get results. You may never have to use a crop, but carry one anyway (a three-foot length of a green branch will serve)—its mere presence induces many horses to behave. Use it firmly but not savagely on the rump immediately after a disobedience, so that Sultan will associate the punishment with the crime. A delay of even a few seconds is too long. Brandishing a crop, however isn't a very useful threat, just a likely way to cause shying or even running away. Spurs belong only on riders who have achieved correct leg position. They are used to reinforce leg signals, never for punishment.

"Walk the first mile out and the last mile in" is an honorable maxim. To return an overheated horse to the barn is thoughtless, as is failing to permit him to warm up before a strenuous trot or canter. You'll find that you'll want to loosen up, too.

Sultan may tend to become skitterish on windy days, an atavism to the era of equine harassment by wolves and other predators, since wind interferes with picking up scent. Hearing is another acute sense. Horse's ears turn toward the object of their attention, and when they are laid flat back it is usually a semaphore signal for kicking or bucking. Should that occur, urge Sultan ahead both as a distraction and to put him out of position to make trouble.

Leave the ring for trail riding only when your instructor thinks you're ready and go with a companion whenever possible. There are traditional "rules of the road" designed for safety and courtesy:

—Look both ways and wait until the coast is clear before crossing a road.

—When riding along a road, stay as far to the right as possible. Never trot or canter on pavement. Signal to oncoming cars to slow down and thank drivers for their courtesy.

*Get a Horse!*

83

—Let anyone with whom you're riding know before you increase speed—don't trot or canter off without warning. Since some horses don't get along well together, be alert for signs of trouble (those ears laid back) and keep your distance.

—Signal a rider whom you want to overtake that you're behind with an audible "Passing, please." It's bad manners just to race by.

—When two riders approach from different directions passing is always done at the slower gait. E.g., if you're trotting and the other rider is walking, you slow down to a walk.

—Advise others of such dangers as holes, broken glass, icy patches, and deep puddles.

—Respect the property of others. Ask permission to ride across private land, close gates behind you, stay away from cultivated fields, and don't trespass on posted land.

Permitting a horse to graze or munch at a passing branch of leaves en route is the way to encourage a bad habit. Besides, the plants may have been sprayed with toxic weed killers.

If you must dismount outside the ring (or at any time, for that matter), slip the reins over your arm. Never let a horse roam free, but don't tie him by the reins, either. Carry a halter if you plan to stop along the way for any substantial length of time.

Just because you've learned to ride doesn't mean that you won't lapse into bad habits. Be aware of your technique and welcome (and heed) criticism from your youngsters and companions.

Above all, remember that exercise should be enjoyable for both horse and rider. Vary gaits and directions in the ring and on the trail, and never ask Sultan to exert himself beyond his limit. The correct amount of daily exercise depends on a combination of a horse's condition and the weather, from a minimum of thirty minutes to several hours for a horse in peak condition. Your vet will prescribe any restrictions when Sultan is suffering or recovering from an ailment. With regard to weather, summer heat is as unbearable to a horse as to us, so lunge or ride during early morning or late evening. Be cautious about riding over frozen ground, it is as harmful to hooves as pavement and just as slippery. Lunging might prove a better idea under such conditions, and whether you conduct your exercise from the saddle or on the ground, use a pick to prevent snow from becoming packed in hooves.

*eight* YOUR

# CHILD AND THE HORSE

## OBSERVATIONS

Once there was a teen-age girl who convinced her parents to keep a horse in the back yard. She was the very paragon of responsibility during the first two months, mucking out the stall, polishing the saddle, and going out riding with a devotion right out of *National Velvet*. But then something happened. The girl's interest began to wane: she found excuses to avoid doing chores, she performed them in a half-hearted, slovenly manner when forced to, and she exercised the animal only when the spirit moved her. Evidence of her neglect included currycombs and brushes strewn around the tack-room floor, the feed barrel left uncovered, and the girl on the telephone when she should have been in the saddle. Her parents found themselves doing a disproportionate amount of work around the barn. Threats, such as "you can't go to the Junior Prom unless your attitude improves, young lady," would result in a few days of adherence to the work schedule but with less enthusiasm than Cinderella showed about sweeping. Then her father had the idea of inviting the girl's former riding instructor to lunch one Saturday, a fellow whom the girl highly respected. Her embarrassment mounted as the instructor cast a baleful eye on the condition of horse and stable, especially when he reminded the girl of her promise to take good care of the animal when she worked to induce her parents to buy it. The reason for the girl's change in attitude came out during lunch: she just assumed that her folks would take care of all the "dirty work"—after all, hadn't they always picked up her toys and clothing? A frank conversation, including some avuncular advice from the instructor to daughter and parents, quickly straightened out matters, whereupon everyone (including the horse) lived happily ever after.

Moral: it's not uncommon for attitudes to change. Children may show all the requisite enthusiasm leading up to buying a horse, yet putting promises and responsibilities into practice can be quite another matter. You as parents should notice whether something's amiss, simply by using your good judgment—horse sense, if you will. A child savagely using crop or spur in the name of "discipline" doesn't look right, and it isn't. Nor is a son bragging about riding the family "bronco" after inserting a burr under its saddle. Someone must look after the horse's well-being in cases of negligence or malevolence, and that person is you. Don't hesitate to use whatever punishment seems intelligent and appropriate, such as depriving the offender of riding or another favorite activity.

A more dangerous and prevalent problem is that of neighborhood children teasing your horse and harassing riders. Often jealous of your youngsters' owning their own horse (or perhaps being just plain cruel), they may throw rocks, swerve bicycles, jump out from behind bushes, or endanger the horse and rider in other ways. Encourage your family to report all such incidents—it's not "tattling"—and call the parents. As a last resort you may have to refer the matter to the police in the event the adults are unable or unwilling to control their children, for such behavior cannot be permitted to continue.

## ESTABLISHING "GROUND RULES"

Impress on your children that it is essential to obey certain "ground rules" whenever they ride off your property. Phrase the rules along the following lines:

—Ride in the company of another person whenever possible. Both of you will be glad for the available assistance if something happens.

—Tell your parents what route you plan to take and approximately how long you'll be away. Telephone in the event you're detained and always carry a couple of dimes for that purpose.

—Avoid riding along or crossing roads as much as possible; detour around built-up areas, construction sites, and any other place where a horse might encounter unnerving sights and sounds.

—Ask permission before riding across someone's land and respect the owner's wishes if he refuses. Make sure gates are securely closed behind you so livestock can't escape.

*Get a Horse!*

—Don't take unnecessary risks, such as jumping across ditches, galloping down steep hills, or trying stunts like "Pony Express" with quick stops and flying dismounts. Anyone who dares you to do them is less of a horseman than he thinks he is.

If your kids start fussing, you can add that even people of Olympic caliber don't take chances. These rules aren't going to inhibit independence or enjoyment; they're designed only to minimize the chance of accidents and injuries which really would restrict your youngsters' riding.


## ACCIDENTS

Accidents are, however, an inevitable part of the sport, and young riders should know how to react. In the event a companion is injured, youngsters should first make sure the person is comfortable, then go for help, either riding home if it's nearby or telephoning parents. Adults will give instructions, usually involving returning to the companion to wait there for help. The injured rider's horse should be caught if it's placidly grazing nearby, though more likely it will have headed home.

And what of the parent whose morning coffee on the patio is interrupted by the sight of a riderless horse trotting back to the barn? First of all, don't panic. Wait to hear from the youngster's companion; if he was riding alone, trace the route he told you he was taking. Perhaps all that's needed is a word of comfort to soothe loss of dignity. If the injury is more serious, apply first aid, a subject with which everyone in the family should be knowledgeable. Three kinds of horse-caused injuries are most prevalent:

—Falls: Someone who has landed hard enough to have the wind knocked out should raise both arms over his head and force himself to breathe. In any event, get up slowly and avoid placing weight on a limb which feels broken. Don't be a hero and try to remount if something hurts—you'll only aggravate the injury. A hot bath and liniment will relieve soreness and stiffness, but caution suggests receiving medical attention in the event of a serious bruise.

—Kicks: Horseshoes can wear down to razor-sharpness, so if a kick breaks the skin, use a piece of clean cloth (a shirt or handkerchief) to stop the flow of blood. A belt or boot garter will serve as a tourniquet in case of profuse bleeding. A cold compress or soaking in water will reduce swelling, then an elastic bandage provides support while a joint is healing (most kicks seem to connect with ankles and knees).

—Bites: Even a playful nip can break the skin. Stop the bleeding, then apply a disinfectant. In that regard, everyone should receive an antitetnus injection and periodic booster shots, for bacteria breeds in manure and flourishes around stables. Many bites occur when feeding sugar lumps and other tidbits. Learn the proper technique: offer the sugar from the flattened palm of the hand, with fingers bent back out of harm's way. Even better, offer the treats in a small pan—Sultan will like you just as much.

In this general area of "child psychology," the role of parents can best be described as supportive. A youngster who has fallen or become injured in another way can become discouraged or reluctant to continue riding. We all know instances of people who stopped riding after a fall—unless there's an injury, encourage the child to remount. But the best "medicine" is preventive: obeying safety rules is the way to reduce chances of accidents and injuries.

*Get a Horse!*

nine CALL

# ME A VET

Somebody once drew a parallel between veterinary medicine and pediatrics: in neither field can patients explain what's bothering them. "Very interesting," you say uninterestedly, until you realize that part and parcel of keeping a horse is looking after him in sickness as well as in health. Your role is not to treat an equine ailment so much as be able to recognize one, an awesome yet wholly manageable responsibility, particularly if one applies the techniques used in raising young children.

## HOW TO KEEP A HORSE HEALTHY

Preventive medicine is an important facet of horse care. As the Royal Canadian Air Force and others teach us, we can feel and look better by keeping physically fit. That also applies to Royal Canadian Mounties' mounts: making sure Sultan receives sensible, regular exercise is the first step in reducing health problems. "Sensible exercise" starts with knowing what a horse's physical limitations are. Race horses can gallop for a mile at top speed; pleasure horses can't, and it's cruel to demand greater speed or distance than Sultan can willingly produce. Weather is also a factor that enthusiastic equestrians all too frequently disregard. To gallop over frozen ground or to canter even casually on a torrid summer day is to invite trouble. Regularity of exercise is equally important. As you learned in Chapter 7 (and it bears repeating), thirty minutes a day is the bare minimum, and twice that is preferable. Skipping a day and riding for two hours the next is not an acceptable compensation.* Of course, neither man nor beast should be expected to venture out in a downpour or blizzard (actually, man still must do the chores), but to pass up exercise because of "something better to do" is irresponsible. Regularity has its practical reasons: a horse that has had even a brief layoff will become fractious the next time out, to the point of throwing a few playful bucks, which are always to be avoided.

Preventive medicine also involves conscientious grooming and the use of good-quality feed. As mentioned earlier, grooming stimulates blood circulation and removes causes of possible infection, while a

* Several horsemen have suggested modifying this sentence, for it is only in the best of all possible worlds that family-owned horses are ridden every day. I would have to agree that a horse can be left in its paddock for a day or even two without any serious deleterious effect. Certainly a few days of rain will prevent exercise, and even Secretariat doesn't receive a daily exercise. What I'm trying to stress is that if you have the chance, daily lunging or riding is better than not. By no means, however, neglect the horse completely. Stalls must be mucked out, and food and water provided.

balanced, appetizing diet is at the heart of any living creature's well-being.

Humans, particularly young ones, receive periodic dental and medical examinations and treatment. So should Sultan. Constant grinding against grain can cause a horse's back teeth to erode into sharp edges. Unless the teeth are filed smooth, by a procedure called "floating," poor Sultan won't feel very much like eating. A vet should check at least every six months to see whether such dental work is necessary. At some point it may be necessary to remove the small "wolf teeth" in the front of Sultan's mouth.

Hooves require more frequent attention. Their outer portions are like our fingernails: hard and nerveless (as demonstrated by their ability to receive and retain horseshoe nails) and constantly growing. The frequency of the blacksmith's visits depends on hooves' condition and rate of growth, normally every four to six weeks to trim hooves and refit shoes, or as soon after you notice Sultan has lost a shoe as he can come. It is unwise to ride a shoeless horse; strain on the bare hoof can cause lameness. Because blacksmiths are among the most overworked if not the rarest of God's creatures, don't expect yours to drop everything and come running as soon as you call. When he makes his periodic visits, be sure someone is at home to meet and assist him, for you can't afford to alienate the chap. Not that you'd want to—some of the most valuable advice a horse-owner will receive can come from a blacksmith. It's hard to go wrong following his suggestions, and he'll be happy to answer any questions, however naïve you may think they are. You'll learn more from listening to a blacksmith as he files a hoof or forges a shoe than any book in the world could impart.

*Get a Horse!*

Additional periodic veterinary care includes an annual tetanus vaccination (as beneficial to Sultan as it is for everyone in the household) and an antiworm preparation mixed in with feed every six months.

Despite all the exercise, care, and medical attention Sultan receives, he wouldn't be equine if he didn't come down with some sort of ailment at some point. In a few instances he'll be able to show you where it hurts—a cut fetlock or a sore leg—but more often he won't. His behavior, however, will indicate that something is wrong, so you must learn to recognize any departures from normal habits.

A healthy horse eats well and looks well, with an alert expression, glossy coat, and lively, unhampered action in his gaits. When Sultan refuses to eat or goes "off his feed," loses weight, develops skin or bone disorders, has loose bowels, moves awkwardly or not at all, he's putting you on notice that something's the matter with him.

## HOW TO RECOGNIZE AILMENTS

A veterinarian whose patients include many family-owned horses and who receives daily calls from perplexed novices recommended that I include a chapter with a chart of symptoms, possible diagnosis, and first-aid advice for the most prevalent of equine ailments. "Immediate treatment" recommends steps to take even before the vet arrives or while someone else is making the phone call to the doctor, who will prescribe additional treatment until he gets there. Implicit in these paragraphs is an injunction to remain calm and professional. A sick horse is uncomfortable enough without having a human on hand to communicate panic as well. The greatest assistance an owner can give a vet is to describe the symptoms as accurately as possible and to mention the horse's recent activities, particularly if there has been any strenuous exercise or change in eating patterns. Two bits of data you should record are breathing and pulse rate: a healthy horse's flanks move eight to twelve times per minute when in repose and the pulse (taken by feeling the large artery under the lower jaw) is thirty-six to forty beats per minute.

## COMMON AILMENTS

*symptoms:* Distended stomach; rolling on the ground; kicking at stomach with hind legs; constantly getting up and lying down; assuming unusual positions (such as trying to sit on its haunches); refusing to eat.

*ailment:* Colic, caused by improperly digested food and resulting gas accumulation (the animal's movements and contortions are attempts to relieve the internal pressure).

*immediate treatment:* Keep him on his feet at all cost—rolling around can cause an inflamed intestine to become twisted. Blanket the horse and walk him slowly around the paddock until the vet arrives.

———

*symptoms:* Unwillingness to place weight on a particular foot; nodding head or pronounced swishing of tail when moving; lumps, swelling, or tenderness on affected foot.

*ailment:* Lameness, caused by strain on or a bruise to a hoof or incorrect shoeing.

*immediate treatment:* Relieve as much weight as possible, to the extent of dismounting and walking back to the barn if the symptoms occur while riding. Gently check the hoof for stones, nails, or other foreign objects (remove them immediately) and for cuts or bruises. Notice whether the horse moves normally after an object has been removed.

———

*symptoms:* A hoof's frog or central area is spongy-soft and tender, emitting pus and a foul odor; the horse refuses to put weight on that leg.

*ailment:* Thrush, an infection caused by excessive contact with moisture, usually in the stall.

*immediate treatment:* Confine the horse on thoroughly dry bedding.

———

*symptom:* A crack or fissure in a hoof.

*ailment:* Cracked hoof, caused by lack of moisture.

*immediate treatments:* If a slight, surface crack, the vet may prescribe over the phone a salvelike dressing. A deeper fissure can require either corrective shoeing or letting the horse go "barefoot" for a while.

———

*symptoms:* Swelling on any part of the leg accompanied by heat (inflammation) and sensitivity to touch; unnatural movement or difficulty in walking.

*ailment:* Curb, capped hock, spavin, or splint. These and other conditions usually result from strains or sprains, overexertion, galloping over hard surfaces, bumps, or falls.

*immediate treatment:* Keep the horse quiet and comfortable; do not place any strain on his back (i.e., do not ride).

———

*symptoms:* Distended, elevated toe (the front part of the hoof); walking on the heel (the rear portion); extreme discomfort and awkwardness while walking; heat throughout the affected legs.

*ailment:* Laminitis (also known as "founder"), always occurring in two or more feet simultaneously. It is an inflammation of the hooves' blood vessels.

*immediate treatment:* Put a blanket on the horse and place affected feet in buckets of cold water or running stream.

---

*symptoms:* Loss of weight although the horse is eating normally; lackluster coat; tightening of skin.

*ailment:* Worms, parasites inhabiting horses' stomachs and intestines.

*immediate treatment:* Keep the horse in his stall with extra-fresh bedding. Remove any fly eggs found on legs or chest by clipping or washing with hot water. Save most recent bowel movements for vet's examination.

---

*symptoms:* Coughing or difficulty in breathing; mucous discharge through nostrils; loss of appetite.

*ailment:* Head cold.

*immediate treatment:* Isolate the horse from other animals. Wipe mucus from nostrils with pieces of clean cloth or cotton, burning them afterward. Put a blanket on the horse and keep him out of drafts.

---

*symptom:* Unusually loose bowel movement.

*ailment:* Diarrhea.

*immediate treatment:* Diarrhea is frequently the symptom of another, more serious illness, so check the horse's general condition carefully. A change in diet, particularly the sudden introduction of fresh grass or green hay, can loosen a horse's stools.

---

*Get a Horse!*

*symptoms:* Cold sweat on a hot day; sluggishness; lying down and refusing to rise.

*ailment:* Exhaustion or sunstroke.

*immediate treatment:* Place the horse in the nearest shade, forcing him to his feet if he tries to lie down. Apply cool (not cold) water over head and body, giving small quantities to drink when the sweating stops.

---

*symptoms:* Bleeding anywhere on head, body, or legs.

*ailment:* Cut or puncture.

*immediate treatment:* Determine the location and severity of the injury. If a minor scrape, wash thoroughly and apply an antiseptic spray. Severe bleeding from a deep cut or puncture can require a piece of rope or cloth as a tourniquet, then use a clean piece of cloth or cotton to staunch the blood flow. In case of nosebleed, press cold compresses only on the outside of the nostrils.

## CARING FOR THE SICK HORSE

Your family's role once the vet arrives is to follow his requests. One of you may be asked to hold Sultan steady, to lead him around the paddock, or all of you may be requested to stay away. Perhaps there is nothing wrong, and the vet will explain where you erred, but if Sultan is sick you will be given detailed instructions for home care.

You may need to take Sultan's temperature. Done rectally, the procedure is easier when two people do it, one preventing the horse from moving around while the other inserts the thermometer and keeps the tail from swishing (stand directly behind the tail as little as possible). Although the family thermometer will serve, a larger and sturdier instrument designed for veterinary use is more practical. In either case, a piece of strong twine tied to the end will facilitate removal. Normal temperature is 100.5°.

Most digestive and related ailments are compounded by the fact that horses are unable to vomit. The fastest way to flush their systems is to give a dose of mineral oil or another purge, something to which Sultan will take as kindly as your children do. The apparatus can be either an enema bag or a plastic garbage bag to which a foot-long piece of rubber or plastic tubing is fastened at the mouth as a nozzle (use a couple of thick rubber bands to secure the tubing). As someone else elevates Sultan's head, insert the nozzle in the corner of the mouth and squeeze out a dose, rubbing the horse's throat to encourage swallowing. The operation will be messy and frustrating, too, since Sultan's reluctance to accept the medicine will cause a goodly portion of the purge to run down his chin, down your arms, and into your face. Do not insert the nozzle between his front teeth or he will be able to bite it off.

Hoof and leg ailments may call for poultice bandages (Figure 16). Burlap or another heavy material can be cut into a sock or boot shape; it's easier to make if you use the bag's corner. Apply the poultice to the hoof, slip on a plastic sandwich bag, then tie the bandage securely around the fetlock. Be on the alert for flying hooves.

The following mixed bag of veterinary advice contains other matters of which you should be aware (again, your vet is the last word):

—Check with your vet whenever anything seems out of the ordinary. Too often an attitude of "maybe

*Get a Horse!*

it'll go away" or "I don't want to bother the doctor" has led to serious complications.

—A tack room should contain a chest or box with the following items: thermometer; clean rags and at least one new towel; antiseptic spray or powder for minor cuts; scissors; Vaseline; and liniment, colic remedy, and laxative as recommended by your veterinarian.

—Hooves showing a tendency toward dryness, especially during very hot or cold weather, can be treated by applying a lubricating dressing daily with a brush.

—Coughing or sneezing without fever or mucus discharge might be caused by an allergy to the bedding. You may have to change the material.

—"Cribbing" is not cheating on a dressage test, but a bad habit some horses have of clenching their teeth on a railing or post, arching their necks, and sucking air into their lungs. Cribbing straps buckle around the neck to make the habit uncomfortable to perform. A reason for cribbing may be boredom, so Sultan may be telling you he'd like more exercise.

—Observe sanitary habits around an ailing horse. Wash your hands and change your clothes after you've finished treating him. Keep other animals away, to prevent infection from spreading and for safety's sake, since an out-of-sorts horse is more likely to kick or bite.

—Ill-fitting blankets, pads, and saddles cause saddle sores. Cutting away a piece of the pad over the affected area can provide relief, together with commercial salves or dressings. Rest may be prescribed as the only remedy in severe cases, with lunging as the only exercise.

—The presence of rodents around a stable is never a good sign. Field mice, chipmunks, and squirrels find spilled grains easy pickings, particularly during win-

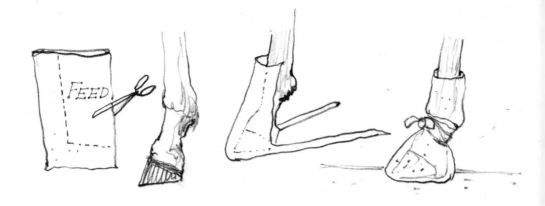

Figure 16

ter months. Check feed and hay for rodent droppings, which can prove fatal if ingested. Pick up any spilled or leftover feed. Cats are wonderful guards: few stables are without one, and horses seem to have a close affinity with felines.

—Finally, always observe your horse critically. Notice how much and how fast he eats, how he moves, and any peculiar traits during normal health so you'll be able to recognize any departures from habit.

Before you race to enroll Sultan for Blue Cross, please be assured that if he gets that combination of preventive medicine and daily care it's unlikely he'll ever suffer from even a handful of the illnesses or conditions described in this chapter. For example, laminitis most frequently results from breaking into a feed bin (odd, isn't it, how overeating can lead to sore feet?), so that checking to make sure the container is securely closed reduces the likelihood of the ailment. Well-fitting tack properly put in place precludes saddle sores, while thrush comes only from a soggy stall and hoof neglect. Your family's conscientious care, an elementary knowledge of equine ailments, and perioidic professional attention will make raising a healthy horse no more difficult than raising a healthy child.

*Get a Horse!*

ten HORSE

# COMMUNES

There's no need to abandon the idea of keeping a horse if you don't have enough land or money, if zoning restrictions prevent it, or if someone in your family is allergic to animals. A viable alternative is to join other families in maintaining a multi-horse facility. This would also solve the problem of stabling a second horse, if space won't permit, or of providing larger surroundings and the company of other equestrians if you've outgrown the back-yard scene.

The first step is to locate other participants. Ask at the riding academies and saddlery shops; inquire of horsy neighbors, the veterinarian, blacksmith, and feed dealer; or place an advertisement in local newspapers. Interview prospective members the same way you would go about finding a roommate or business partner. You (together with members acquired along the way) must be completely satisfied that any rider has the requisite ability, and that both youngsters and parents are keenly interested and have a sense of responsibility. Vets, blacksmiths, and riding instructors given as references should unhesitatingly confirm these qualities and indicate whether the horses to become tenants have or have had any recurring communicable diseases. The number of humans involved is less important than the number of animals. A maximum of six horses is recommended, for more than that number can prove unmanageable for an amateur operation. Unless you want to hear the patter of little hooves around the barn, exclude stallions if someone owns a mare. Finally, it makes sense to choose people whom everyone else knows and likes and who live in the neighborhood.

The newly formed commune's initial collective task is to look for land. Approach owners whose property includes a stable with several vacant stalls or a farmer with space in his barn (he might be glad to have the additional income). You'll have to start from scratch if there's no existing building, so check out spare fields or unused acreage on farms and estates (perhaps their owners might even want to join your venture). The kind of land needed is the same as for a back-yard facility except as otherwise noted in this chapter; Chapters 1 and 2 will give you the particulars. For safety and security the barn should be within eyesight of someone's house. Don't forget to check zoning restrictions to see if there are any limits as to the number of horses allowed for each acre on otherwise acceptable sites.

Having located a suitable place, the commune should then work out a lease with the landowner. Ask

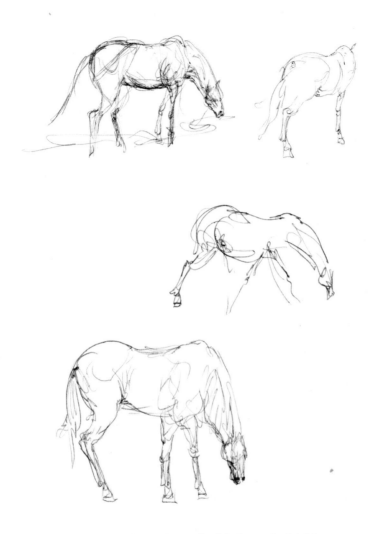

him to grant you the right to build (or refurbish) stables, paddocks, and a ring and the right to maintain
horses on the land. Ownership of the building and ring
is a matter for negotiation. Rent should be based on
the number of animals not on a fixed monthly sum;
there's no hard-and-fast rule—try for $20 to $30 per
house per month based on five or six occupied stalls.
All members must sign the agreement, since they will
all share the expense of construction and maintenance,

*Get a Horse!*

and indemnify the landowner against any damages and injuries to his property and family.

Members' duties and obligations toward the venture and one another must also be set forth in a written agreement, which should include the following provisions:

—Responsibilities for chores will be performed according to a schedule to which all the parties agree to adhere unless otherwise revised.

—All expenditures, including initial construction and furnishing, together with ongoing feed, bedding, and maintenance costs, will be borne equally (pro rata in the event a member owns more than one horse). A member who is appointed treasurer will be responsible for paying the bills (the treasurer may want to set up a separate checking account into which members deposit estimated monthly shares).

—Veterinary and blacksmith bills are the individual obligation of the owner of the horse so treated, as would be compensation for damage caused by the horse or the owner's negligence (the latter clause guards against you having to pay for damage caused by another member's forgetting to lock the stall door and allowing his horse to trample the owner's flower bed).

—A member can permit a guest to ride another member's horse only with prior permission. The member-host is responsible for injuries to the guest or the borrowed horse.

—A horse deemed by a veterinarian to have contracted a communicable disease will be immediately isolated from the other horses (where?—the owner's problem; perhaps to someone's back yard) and will indemnify other owners for any expenses caused by the ailment. (This clause encourages an owner to remove an infected horse before others can become infected.)

—A member who fails to carry out his obligations, such as performing or overseeing chores, may be voted out of the venture by a majority of the other members, his liability terminating only upon payment of any outstanding sums (the rest of you have guarded against having to assume his share of expenses by paying rent on a per-horse basis).

—Anyone choosing to withdraw from the venture may assign his membership only to a party whom the remaining members have unanimously approved.

So much for paperwork and on to construction. Stalls can be either separate adjacent units or a single building (Figures 17a and 17b). The advantage of the latter is that everything is under one roof, making chores easier. Partitions between stalls should be at least four feet high so that a horse can see (or sense) his neighbors, yet is unable to bite or scavenge feed.

Stalls and the feed room–tack room require the same furnishings found in a single-horse barn. The tack room needs a rack for each saddle, bridle, and halter, along with plenty of shelving and cabinet space for grooming implements and medicine. Communal economics come into play in such matters as one wheelbarrow for the entire facility, a cheaper-by-the-dozen package of sponges, and one large-economy-size jar of saddle soap. Use your collective good sense in determining which items can be shared without inconvenience and bad feelings, then be sure that individually owned things are clearly identified.

The paddock should be as large as possible, for the simple reason that damage to turf increases with the number of animals. A single area works in most cases, but be prepared to subdivide in the event two or more horses don't get along. Horses develop their own pecking order for water troughs and patches of ground:

*Get a Horse!*

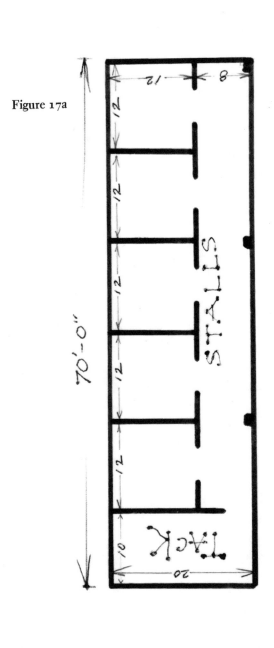

Figure 17a

70'-0"

12 12 12 12 12 12 8

STALLS

20 10

TACK

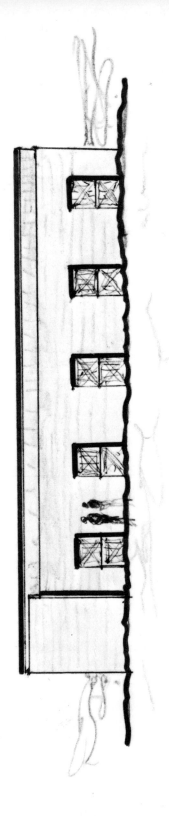

*Get a Horse!*

110

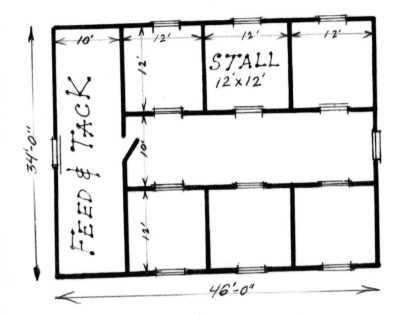

Figure 17b

keep your eye out for newcomers being harassed by older residents and try to break up any skirmishes that may occur around feeding time.

A 150-by-100-foot ring reduces the chances of riders trodding on each others' heels. A nearby meadow or trail adds variety, and try to get the use of available land across which you can blaze a bridle path. First obtain the landowner's written permission to construct one and the right to ride across his property. Avoid areas frequented by hunters (they'll shoot at anything that moves), creek beds which become filled after rainstorms, and any stretch of perpetually soggy ground. Design the route so you won't have to chop down trees. The path should be 8 to 10 feet wide at its narrowest points, and marked by arrows painted on trees.

The manure pit should have a 10-foot diameter. If one proves inadequate, build another.

*Get a Horse!*

**111**

Finally, order the feed and bedding. Since there's usually a discount in buying these items in bulk, feel free to negotiate with the dealers, especially if there is more than one supplier in your locale.

The heart of any communal effort is the participation of every member. Assuming there are to be six families involved, named White, Black, Green, Brown, Gray, and You, a schedule for the supervision of morning and evening chores might be as follows:

|  | Sun. | Mon. | Tues. | Wed. | Thurs. | Fri. | Sat. |
|---|---|---|---|---|---|---|---|
| A.M. | White | Green | Black | Brown | Gray | You | Green |
| P.M. | You | Brown | Gray | Green | White | Black | Green |

A family which lives very near the barn, such as the Greens, can easily appear on the chart most frequently, and accordingly receive a concession for their presence when it comes time to pay bills. An alternative to this schedule is that families can pair off: White and Green, Brown and Black, and Gray and You. Each team is "on" every third day, deciding between itself which partner will be there for morning and which for evening chores. These schedules don't mean, however, that the family must perform everyone else's chores; it merely designates responsibility for presence. Even though youngsters can be assigned the tasks of feeding, watering, and mucking out, at least one adult must be available to inspect the premises during evening chores, making certain that stall and paddock gates are locked. Exercise does not appear on the schedule, since it must be assumed that each horse will be ridden or lunged every day by its owner.

Families can swap assignments just as individuals can in a back-yard situation, yet exchanges should take place only for very sound reasons to avoid unpleasantness and accusations of shirking. A group meeting is useful to talk about organizational problems and to

*Get a Horse!*

iron out personality conflicts. Deal promptly with any friction over missing assignments, failure to pay bills promptly, or neglect of others' (or even one's own) horses before irreconcilable differences erupt. A veterinarian is the appropriate arbitrator of matters involving equine health. Although differences of opinion are inevitable, if you and the other participants keep the communal spirit in mind and demonstrate your shared enthusiasm for horses and riding, the venture can't help but be successful and enjoyable.

*Get a Horse!*

eleven GROU

# ACTIVITIES

Anyone who has ever joined a friend for a hack along a bridle path, belonged to a horse-owners' commune, or just watched a busy stable knows there's more to riding than one rider on one horse in one back yard. The sport is a naturally sociable pastime, so joining others is a sure way to increase everyone's enjoyment, regardless of which member of the family is on Sultan's back.

## HORSE SHOWS

Put two riders together and sooner or later competition rears its head, especially among junior equestrians. A horse show (call it a rodeo if you're partial to

Western-style riding) is a natural outlet for this sort of rivalry. Riders who aren't quite ready to match their skills at more formal shows can stage one of their own with neighbors or other commune members. Select a time and place (with an alternate date in case of rain) six or eight weeks in advance, then invite riders of approximately the same ability to enter. Once you know how many there will be, determine the number and type of individual events, called classes: perhaps equitation (walk, trot, and canter) and Western horsemanship (walk, jog, and lope). A dollar or two as entry fee for each class will go toward paying for colored prize ribbons available from saddlery shops. Order enough so that one will go to each competitor in all classes. Ask your vet or blacksmith to suggest someone to serve as judge, a person with sufficient impartiality and expertise. Type up a program several days before the show. Each entrant should be assigned a number, and the program should indicate the classes and competitors' names and numbers. Mimeograph or Xerox the sheet, making enough copies for participants and spectators. You'll also need to make identifying numerals which entrants will wear safety-pinned to their backs. Cut heavy white cardboard into ten-inch circles and use a felt-tipped pen to write the numbers.

Expect well-groomed horses and well-turned-out (and nervous) contestants on the day of the show. An adult should serve as ringmaster to assist the judge; the basic job is to instruct entrants when to change gaits or directions. An announcer with a bullhorn or a portable public-address system can call the classes and announce the winners. Ask the judge to explain to participants the reasons for his decisions in equitation classes as a clue to future improvement. Parents should be prepared to cheer up disappointed losers in a spirit of "better luck next time" rather than "sour grapes." Don't forget to thank the judge after the show (a bottle of liquor or good wine is an appropriate honorarium).

GAMES

As part of the show or as a separate event, gymkhana games are fun to play and to watch. They are activities which demonstrate coordination between horse and rider as well as the latter's skills. The most popular games are:

—Egg Balance: Riders balance eggs on soup spoons as they walk, then trot around the ring. The winner is the last person to drop the egg.

—Tacking: At the word "go" contestants lead their horses by halters to the far end of the ring where their tack awaits. The one who bridles and saddles his horse, then rides back to the starting line first, is the winner.

—Barrel Race: Entrants individually race around three barrels or bales of hay, tracing the cloverleaf pattern indicated in Figure 18. The fastest time determines the winner; going off course results in disqualification, and knocking down a barrel or a bale adds ten penalty seconds to one's time. Remind riders that horses can lose their balance by taking tight turns at the canter on incorrect leads.

—Musical Chairs: The familiar game of one-fewer-chair-than-players. When music provided by a portable radio, tape recorder, or phonograph stops, trotting or cantering riders dismount and lead their horses to the nearest empty folding chair. The last remaining competitor is the winner.

Highlights of both horse shows and gymkhanas are

*Get a Horse!*

**Figure 18**

costume classes and musical rides. The former involves a parade of horses and riders in costumes based on a predetermined category, such as historical or literary figures, or television or comic-strip characters. Awards go to the ones showing the most imagination and best execution. A musical ride makes an exciting exhibition. A minimum of six riders should plan and rehearse to taped martial music a routine of circles, serpentines, and figure-eights at the walk, trot, and canter in single file and pairs. A ride of about ten minutes is enough to avoid repeating figures. Members of the mounted unit will look more professional in "uniforms" of matching shirts or sweaters, as will horses wearing mane and tail ribbons of the same color.

At some point your youngsters may want to supplement this home entertainment by competing in shows or rodeos staged at local stables. The role of parents usually is to pay entry and transportation fees, and certainly to help give Sultan an extra-special grooming for the event. Everyone naturally will want to attend and root for their relatives. Don't, however, be a "stage mother" by pushing unwilling children into competition, berating them for poor showings, or informing a judge that he made a bad decision. With regard to rodeos, you may have to put your foot down in the event an enthusiastic son signs up for bronc-riding or steer-wrestling (although some Western high schools and colleges offer rodeo as a well-supervised intramural activity). Firmly suggest calf-roping as an alternative if Sultan has been trained for that event.

## OTHER ACTIVITIES

Fox hunting is no longer the province of the landed gentry or people who don't mind risking a broken neck jumping over fences or across ditches.* All the sport requires is a sound horse (it doesn't even have to jump—there's no shame in going around an obstacle) and an enthusiasm for cross-country riding. Friends who belong to a local hunt will give your kids all the necessary details about this tradition-bound sport where the courtesies required may, if you're lucky, carry over to the family dinner table. Whoever feeds the horse on the morning of a hunt should allow at least two hours for him to digest his breakfast.

Two activities out of Sultan's league (and more than likely his riders') are endurance rides and racing. Lasting over several days, the former take place over distances up to one hundred miles. It's therefore unfair to ask a horse which hasn't been trained for such a grueling event to compete in one. Racing doesn't just mean showing up at Saratoga or Santa Anita. Any all-

---

* People who disapprove of blood sports might bear in mind that hunting is still a form of predator control and that the fox stands a real chance of escaping; if these two arguments are unconvincing, there are drag hunts, where hounds pursue only a trail of scent.

*Get a Horse!*

out gallop can prove damaging in a variety of ways, the most obvious being strain on wind and legs or a fall from stepping in a hidden hole. Any riding with (or against) others must always be tempered by the realization that Sultan is an amateur athlete, too. No one in your family could play professional football or run a marathon distance, so don't demand that your horse overextend himself in analogous ways.

## USING A TRAILER

Group activities which take place beyond hacking distance from your barn raise the question of how to get your horse there from here. The answer is a trailer hitched to your car or station wagon. Trailers come in a range of models priced according to size and durability. Since a new one is a considerable investment, look for a used trailer in good condition. Many are offered at between $250 and $500, and the expense can be further reduced by sharing a two-horse model with another family or by making it a commune asset. Check ads in local papers and horse magazines and on riding-academy and saddlery-shop bulletin boards; vets and blacksmiths are, as always, excellent sources of information.

Safety and comfort are essential criteria. A two-axle trailer is steadier than the single-axle kind. Sturdy floorboards, especially if made of wood, are as important as in a stall: check under mats and beneath the vehicle for signs of rotting. Look closely at the roof, side panels, and ramp. Inadequate ventilation can turn a trailer into a summer sauna for Sultan, but openings shouldn't let rain blow in. Once again, rely on the expertise of others by asking a garage mechanic to pass judgment on the hitch and safety chain, lights, and tires (don't overlook a spare). Once you've found a likely choice at a reasonable price, the mechanic or seller can show you how to connect the trailer to your car. Let someone else drive while you ride in the trailer to double-check the ventilation and freedom from exhaust fumes. It won't be a cushiony ride— trailers bounce, and a human is considerable less ballast than a half-ton animal. Then if the vehicle passes muster, try some of that horse-tradin' bargaining to reduce the seller's asking price.

The new purchase must be thoroughly cleaned, with all traces of hay and grain eliminated. Replace worn floor mats and padding: old mattresses or thick quilts hung on the walls and both sides of a two-horse trailer's partition will reduce bumps and bruises. Make sure the back panel's bolts are securely tightened, and cover restraining chains with pieces of rubber tubing.

Practice driving your car with the empty rig attached, both forward and in reverse. Items to remember are: start and stop gradually, don't make turns too sharply, use an extended rear-view mirror mounted on the driver's side, and leave enough room for the trailer as you pass another vehicle.

Some horses balk at being loaded or refuse outright to enter a trailer. A lump of sugar or a carrot may entice Sultan up the ramp, and another horse already inside can be reassuring. One reason for recalcitrance frequently is a distrust of the ramp: rubber matting or the kind of cross-strips found on gangplanks will give greater traction than a bare board or panel. Showing your annoyance or frustration will just cause Sultan to balk even more. As a last resort, get two other people to help you. As someone leads the horse toward the trailer, the other two press a wide strap against

*Get a Horse!*

Figure 19

Sultan's rump, watching out for kicking or rearing (Figure 19). Once inside, fasten the animal by a three-foot length of stout rope or chain snapped to his halter and to the ring on the vehicle's front wall.

An uneasy horse can be reassured if you let it stand inside the stationary trailer for short periods of time, then taking the first few trips with a human or another horse as companion and comforter. Drivers will find that the additional weight makes a difference in maneuvering. As in any horse-related activity, the best general rule is to take it slow and easy.

# AFTERWORD

Take a look at that patch of land in your back yard or across the road. Just six months ago it was bare and unused—now there's a barn, paddock, ring, and a horse. Sultan has certainly enhanced your family's existence. Your youngsters ride every day, do their chores, and because of the horse they have shown an increased sense of responsibility. Look at yourself, too. Your knowledge of horses was once limited to Western movies and pitching horseshoes, yet now you can feed, groom, muck out, and in emergencies play "Florence Martingale" to an ailing animal. Why, you can even ride! Feel pleased about it all, you should indeed, but you've only scratched the surface.

The following list of periodicals, books, and organizations will provide comprehensive and timely information about keeping and enjoying a horse on a more sophisticated level. Off you go, and happy riding!

PERIODICALS

There are four well-known national magazines which together encompass all aspects of the horse world:

*American Horseman* (monthly): Articles of general interest on English- and Western-style riding. $1.00 per copy or $12.00 per year: 222 Park Avenue South, New York, New York 10003.

*The Chronicle of the Horse* (weekly): News of horse shows, racing, hunting, and polo. Necessary for participants and wish-fulfillment for the amateur rider/reader. Fifty cents per copy or $15.00 per year: Berryville, Virginia.

*Practical Horseman* (monthly): Articles and columns containing useful information on caring for and training horses. Seventy-five cents per copy or $5.00 per year: 17 W. Miner St., West Chester, Pennsylvania 19380.

*Western Horseman* (monthly): Interesting historic and current material on rodeo, ranching, trail riding, and other subjects on Western-style riding. Sixty cents per copy or $5.00 per year: 3850 North Nevada Avenue, Colorado Springs, Colorado 80901.

*Get a Horse!*

## BOOKS

The first five titles expand much of the basic advice and information you've found here (the first three describe activities for intermediate and advanced riders):

*A Horse Around the House* by Patricia Jacobson and Marcia Hayes (Crown Publishers, Inc.).

*A Horse of Your Own* by M. A. Stoneridge (Doubleday).

*The Horseman's Bible* by J. C. Coggins (Doubleday).

*Top-Form Book of Horse Care* by Frederick Harper (Popular Library).

*So Your Kids Want a Pony* by Joanne Forbes (Stephen Greene Press).

*Make the Most of Your Horse* by Jan Dickerson (Doubleday) explains in a clear fashion the reasons for using weight and balance in riding. A good jumping-off place to the vast literature of horsemanship.

*Gymkhana Games* by Natlee Kenoyer (Stephen Greene Press) contains over sixty competitions, with diagrams and rules.

In addition, ask your vet, your youngsters' instructor, and horsy friends to recommend books on subjects in which your family's riders are involved.

*Get a Horse!*

# ORGANIZATIONS

These organizations will provide information about their respective breeds, registries, and names of local breeders:

*America Connemara Pony Society*, Balston Spa, New York 12020.

*American Quarter Horse Association*, 2736 West 10 Street, Amarillo, Texas 79102.

*American Saddle Horse Breeders Association*, 929 South 4 Street, Louisville, Kentucky 40203.

*American Shetland Pony Club*, Lafayette, Indiana 47902.

*Appaloosa Horse Club*, Box 640, Moscow, Idaho 83843.

*Arabian Horse Club Registry of America*, 120 S. La Salle Street, Chicago, Illinois 60603.

*Morgan Horse Club*, Box 2157, Bishop's Corner Branch, West Hartford, Connecticut 06117.

*Palomino Horse Breeders of America*, P.O. Box 249, Mineral Wells, Texas 76067.

*Pinto Horse Association of America*, Box 155, RFD 1, Ellington, Connecticut 06029.

*Tennessee Walking Horse Breeders and Exhibitors Association of America*, Box 87, Lewisburg, Tennessee 37091.

*Welsh Pony Society of America*, 202 North Church Street, West Chester, Pennsylvania 19380.

*Get a Horse!*

4-H riding clubs are open to youngsters between nine and nineteen who own their own horses. Members receive stable management and riding instruction. Encourage your children to participate in a group if there's one in your area; contact the local Department of Agriculture County Extension Agent for details.

United States Pony Clubs provide hunter-seat equitation instruction and related activities (on either ponies or horses). Contact the U.S. Pony Club, Dover, Massachusetts 02030, for particulars.

# GLOSSARY

A horse's manner or way of moving, especially with re-   *action*
gard to the height it lifts its legs.

A horse nine years or older.   *aged*

Devices by which a rider signals a horse. They include   *aids*
voice, hands, legs, crops, and spurs.

A breed characterized by small dots on its coat at the   *Appaloosa*
hindquarters.

The portion of the foreleg from the elbow to the chest.   *\*arm*

Coloration consisting of any shade of brown coat and   *bay*
black mane and tail.

* Entries illustrated on page 36.

*barrel   The portion of the body around the ribs.

bit   A device, usually metal, fitted into the horse's mouth and used for control.

blaze   A white stripe extending the length of the muzzle.

body brush   A brush with firm, but not stiff, bristles.

box stall   A roomy, square-shaped stall.

bran   The husk of certain grains, used as a laxative and to aid digestion.

breed   Any strain or type of animal whose members can reproduce the characteristics by which the group is defined.

bridle   A leather apparatus fitting over a horse's head to which the bit and reins are attached.

buckskin   Coloration consisting of a tan or light-brown coat with black mane, tail, legs, and a stripe along the spine.

*cannon   The foreleg bone extending from knee to fetlock.

canter   A three-beat gait.

cantle   The rear part of a saddle.

cast   Of a horse, unable to rise to its feet.

cavesson   The noseband of a bridle.

chestnut   Coloration consisting of light-brown coat, mane, and tail. Also, a horny bump on the inside of a horse's legs.

Get a Horse!

The girth strap on a Western saddle used to hold the saddle in place. *cinch*

Any of the events in a horse show. *class*

A gastric disorder, usually the result of improper digestion. *colic*

| | |
|---|---|
| *collection* | The attitude of a horse in motion, during which he is in balance and responsive to the rider's commands. A "collected" trot, for example, is a gentle, slow but animated form of the gait, as opposed to an "extended" trot in which legs and neck reach out in a faster movement. |
| *conformation* | The over-all structure of a horse; the way it is put together. |
| *Connemara* | A breed of pony. |
| *\*coronet* | The portion of the pastern immediately above the hoof. |
| *cribbing* | A habit of biting on wood and sucking air into the lungs. |
| *crop* | A short whip or riding bat having a loop at its lower end. |
| *crossbred* | The offspring of parents of different breeds. |
| *\*croup* | The upper portion of the back from the loins to the dock. |
| *curb* | A bit used primarily to control speed. |
| *curry (verb)* | To comb or brush a horse's coat. |
| *currycomb* | A metal plate with teeth on one side used to clean brushes. |
| *dandy brush* | A brush with stiff bristles. |

*Get a Horse!*

The root of the tail.                                    *dock*

The upper joint of the foreleg.                          *elbow*

1. A general term for riding.                            equitation
2. A horse-show class where only the rider's skills are
judged, not the horse's conformation or performance.

*Get a Horse!*

*ewe neck*   A conformation fault in which the horse's neck is wider at the top than at the base.

*extension*   See "collection."

*\*fetlock*   The joint between the cannon and the pastern.

*filly*   A female horse below the age of four.

*\*flank*   The portion of the body below the loins and behind the barrel.

*float (verb)*   To file down a horse's teeth.

*forelock*   The portion of the mane extending between the ears.

*forequarters*   The portion of the horse in front of the barrel.

*forward seat*   A technique of English-style riding in which the rider keeps his weight over the horse's withers; also known as hunt seat, it is used for jumping.

*founder*   See "laminitis."

*frog*   The soft midsection of the hoof's underpart.

*gait*   Any of the horse's paces. The walk, trot, and canter are the three natural gaits.

*gallop*   A fast canter.

*\*gaskin*   Muscular development along the upper portions of the hind legs.

*gelding*   A castrated male horse.

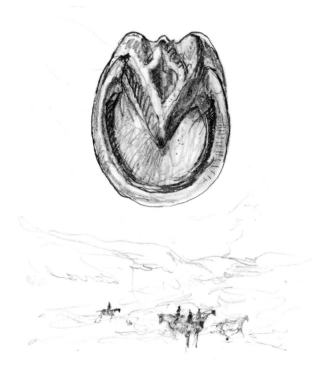

1. The strap that holds the saddle in place.     *girth*
2. The horse's circumference, measured behind the
withers.

A horse or pony which is not a member of any specific    *grade*
breed or type, analogous to a canine "mutt."

*Get a Horse!*

**137**

| | |
|---|---|
| *grain* | Any of the cereals used as feed. As a verb, to feed grain to a horse. |
| *gray* | Colorations consisting of both black-and-white hairs. |
| *gymkhana* | A program of mounted games. |
| *hackamore* | A bitless bridle. |
| *halfbreed* | The offspring of a Thoroughbred and another breed. |
| *hand* | The unit of measuring the height of a horse. One hand equals four inches. |
| *hay* | Dried grass used as feed. |
| *head-shy* | A horse afraid of abuse or pain to its head. |
| *hindquarters* | The portion of the horse behind the barrel. |
| *\*hock* | The lower joint of the hind leg. |
| *\*hoof* | The foot's hard outer covering. |
| *hoof-pick* | An implement used to clean the inside of the hoof. |
| *horse* | 1. A member of the species *Equus caballus*. 2. A male horse over the age of three. |
| *hunt seat* | See "forward seat." |
| *irons* | Another term for English-style stirrups. |
| *jodhpurs* | A variety of pants which extend to the ankles, worn for English-style riding. |

Pollack '73

The lower joint of the foreleg.      *knee

An inflammation of the hoof's inner wall (also known   *laminitis*
as founder).

The sequence of a horse's legs during the canter, de-   *lead* (*noun*)
scribing which foreleg first strikes the ground.

*Get a Horse!*

*lead line*   A rope or chain attached to a halter, with which a horse is led.

*leathers*   Straps supporting the stirrups on an English saddle.

*loins*   The portion of the back on either side of the spine behind the withers.

*lope*   A Western term for canter.

*lunging*   Exercising a horse from the ground whereby the animal circles around and is controlled by means of a long rope.

*mane*   The long hair growing from the top of a horse's neck.

*mare*   A female horse over the age of three.

*martingale*   A piece of tack used to restrain a horse's head elevation.

*Morgan*   A breed used for riding, driving, and pulling.

*muck out*   To remove waste matter from a stall.

*near*   The left side of a horse.

*neck-rein (verb)*   To guide a horse by means of rein pressure against its neck.

*noseband*   The part of a bridle placed above the horse's nostrils; the cavesson.

*off*   The right side of a horse.

*Paint*   See "Pinto."

*Get a Horse!*

A breed or type characterized by a gold-colored coat *Palomino*
and white mane and tail.

The portion of the leg between the fetlock and coro- *pastern*
net.

*Get a Horse!*

*pelham*  A bit composed of a curb and snaffle.

*Pinto*  A breed or type characterized by large patches of color on its coat (also known as Paint).

*\*poll*  The portion of the head between the ears.

*pommel*  The front part of a saddle.

*pony*  A member of a breed or type of small horse, generally standing under 14.2 hands high.

*post (verb)*  In English-style riding, to rise and fall in the saddle at each step of the trot; posting makes the gait more comfortable for the rider.

*poultice*  A salve applied to cure sore legs and hooves.

*Quarter Horse*  A breed associated with Western-style riding and ranch work.

*reins*  Leather straps attached to a bit by which the rider guides and controls the horse.

*roach (verb)*  To cut off or clip a mane.

*roan*  Coloration composed of any solid-colored coat interspersed with white hairs.

*saddle*  A leather apparatus strapped to a horse's back, on which the rider sits.

*Saddle Horse*  A breed used primarily for exhibition in three- and five-gaited classes.

| | |
|---|---|
| A style of English-style riding in which the rider sits back in the saddle in order to display the foreleg action of Saddle Horses. | *saddle-seat* |
| A breed of pony. | *Shetland* |
| The point where the foreleg joins the body. | *\*shoulder* |
| A bit used primarily to control direction. | *snaffle* |
| A Western term for chestnut. | *sorrel* |
| Describing a horse free from blemishes or ailments: one in good health and condition. | *sound* |
| Any of several diseases of the hock. | *spavin* |
| A breed developed for harness (trotting and pacing) racing. | *Standardbred* |
| A Western-style saddle with a horn at the pommel and a high cantle. | *stock saddle* |
| The upper joint of the hind leg. | *\*stifle* |
| The apparatus attached to the saddle in which a rider places his feet. | *stirrup* |
| A strap placed over the girth and saddle to prevent the saddle from slipping. | *surcingle* |
| A collective term for saddles, bridles, and harness. | *tack* |
| A breed noted for its comfortable walk and canter. | *Tennessee Walking Horse* |

*Get a Horse!*

| | |
|---|---|
| *Thoroughbred* | A breed developed for turf racing, also used as hunters and jumpers. |
| *throatlatch* | The part of a bridle that buckles under the neck. |
| *thrush* | An inflammation of the frog. |
| *trot* | A two-beat gait. |
| *Welsh Mountain* | A breed of pony. |
| *\*withers* | The point where the neck joins the top of the body. |
| *wolf teeth* | Small teeth which appear in front of the first molars, often removed if they interfere with the bit. |